THIRD EDITION

DOCUMENTATION in COUNSELING RECORDS

An Overview of Ethical, Legal, and Clinical Issues

Robert W. Mitchell, ACSW

D1089515

AMERICAN COUNSELING ASSOCIATION
5999 Stevenson Avenue
Alexandria, VA 22304
www.counseling.org

THIRD EDITION

DOCUMENTATION
in
COUNSELING
RECORDS

An Overview of Ethical, Legal, and Clinical Issues

10 9 8 7 6 5 4 3 2 1

AMERICAN COUNSELING ASSOCIATION
5999 Stevenson Avenue, Alexandria, VA 22304

DIRECTOR OF PUBLICATIONS   Carolyn C. Baker

PRODUCTION MANAGER   Bonny E. Gaston

COPY EDITOR   Christine Calorusso

EDITORIAL ASSISTANT   Catherine A. Brumley

Cover and text design by Bonny E. Gaston.

LIBRARY OF CONGRESS CATALOGING-IN-PUBLICATION DATA
   Mitchell, Robert, 1937–
Documentaltion in counseling records: an overview of ethical, legal, and clinical issues/by Robert, Mitchell.—3rd ed.
   p. cm.
   Includes bibliographical references.
   ISBN 13: 978-1-55620-273-5 (alk. paper)
   ISBN 10: 1-55620-273-3 (alk. paper)
1. Mental health counseling. 2. Psychiatric social work. 3. Medical records—Law and legislation. I. American Counseling Association. II. Title.
   [DNLM: 1. Medical History Taking—methods—United States—Legislation. 2. Counseling—United States—Legislation. 3. Ethics, Professional—United States—Legislation. 4. Medical Records—United States—Legislation. WB 290 M681d 2006]

RC466.M57 2006
362.2'04256—dc22   2006027652

Dedication

This book is for every person who ever tried to help someone.
Each of you makes a difference.
You always have and you always will.

Contents

Preface ix

About the Author xv

Special Thanks xix

Glossary xxi

CHAPTER 1

Ethical Behavior, Values, and Professional Standards 1

Ethical Conduct 1

Enforceable and Aspirational Guidelines 5

CHAPTER 2

A Legal Perspective 9

Credentials 10

Charting Essentials 10

Testimony and Documentation 12

Missing and Incomplete Entries 16

Altered Documentation 16

The Record as Legal Defense 17

Eight Ways to Guarantee a Lawsuit or
Allegations of Unethical Conduct 18

CHAPTER 3

A Fiscal Perspective 19

What Not to Do 21

What You Must Do 21

Essential Elements for the Staff Note 23

Guidelines for Ethical Billing 25

CHAPTER 4
A Coworker's Perspective   27
   Conclusionary Terms, Modifiers,
      and Abbreviations   28
   Problematic Staff Notes   29
   Possible Repercussions   30
   Clear, Accurate Staff Notes   31

CHAPTER 5
A Client's Perspective   35
   Double Standards   36
   Cultural Diversity   37

CHAPTER 6
Online Counseling and Electronic Records   41
   Online Counseling Services and Safeguards   42
   Electronic Record-Keeping Guidelines   45

CHAPTER 7
Sexual Relationships and Dual Relationships   53
   Sexual Relationships and Ethical Conduct   53
   Dual Relationships in the Counseling Process   57

CHAPTER 8
Documenting High-Risk Cases   61
   Qualifiers, Violence, and Threats of Violence   62
   Homicidal and Suicidal Clients   62
   Physical and Sexual Abuse   65
   Criminal Behavior   65
   Permission for Service Form   66
   Additional Considerations   67
   Need for Specificity   69

CHAPTER 9
Terminations   73
   The Termination Letter   74
   The Termination Summary   75
   Abandonment   76
   Right to Refuse Service   78

Frequently Asked Questions About Documentation   81

Multiple Uses of a Record   81

Subpoenaed Records   82

The Unofficial Chart   82

Brochures and Informational Flyers   83

Preprinted Forms   84

Client's Use of Slang and Vulgar Language   84

Faxed Client Information   85

Terminations and Nonpayment   85

Missing or Lost Documentation   86

Filing Systems and Security   87

Cosignatures, Credentials, Students
and Volunteers   88

HIV/AIDs   89

Disclaimer Forms   91

HIPAA Basics   92

Risk Exposure   94

What Would You Do?: Ethical Considerations   95

Scenarios for Discussion and
Professional Development   95

Six Steps for the Resolution of Ethical Problems   99

Concluding Thoughts   100

Epilogue: You Make a Difference   101

References, Suggested Readings, and Web Sites   105

Preface

In 2005, the American Counseling Association published its revised *Code of Ethics* as approved by the ACA Governing Council. This is the first revision of the Association's *Code of Ethics* since July 1, 1995, and it establishes critical new guidelines for professional conduct.

Documentation in Counseling Records: An Overview of Ethical, Legal, and Clinical Issues (3rd ed.) is written to help counselors reflect on the specific requirements of their profession in light of the new code. The previous two editions, published in 1991 and 2001, focused primarily on the legal dimensions of documentation in the counseling professions. In response to the new code, this third edition builds on that focus but with an emphasis on ethical conduct.

In an age of legal, clinical, and fiscal accountability, record keeping and ethical conduct are important components of professional counseling. As counselors provide services in the 21st century, we must accept reality, and the reality is this:

- Lawsuits and allegations of unethical conduct against counselors continue to increase. Without adequate documentation and adherence to the *ACA Code of Ethics* a counselor's vulnerability is also increased.
- Counselors, client records, and personnel files will continue to be ordered into courtrooms because the legal system believes the documentation contains information needed to make decisions about child custody, involuntary hospitalization, and a wide array of other situations, including allegations of

unethical behavior. Lack of integrity and incompetence as well as missing, incomplete, and inadequate charts can be harmful to the client as well as the counselor.

- There will be occasions when the primary counselor will be sick, on vacation, or otherwise unavailable to provide emergency service. Someone else will depend on the chart to make clinical decisions. Adequate records can ensure appropriate intervention and continuity of care as directed by the *ACA Code of Ethics.*

- All funding sources are demanding documentation that verifies the need for and the rendering of reimbursable activity, as well as verification of counselor competence and accurate billing procedures.

- Utilization reviews, peer reviews, quality assurance reviews, and committees on ethical inquiries will continue to be important parts of professional counseling. An accurate, comprehensive record, as well as an accurate, comprehensive personnel file, will be primary source documents.

This edition emphasizes professional values as an important way of living out an ethical commitment and reinforces the fact that "inherently held values . . . guide our behaviors [and] are deeply ingrained in the counselor and developed out of personal dedication, rather than the mandatory requirement of an external organization" (*ACA Code of Ethics,* Preamble).

The volume, therefore, has a number of key purposes:

- To understand the multiple uses of a record, those who have access to it, and its relationship to the *ACA Code of Ethics*

- To increase awareness of legal trends, the changing definition of confidentiality, and the most frequent causes for malpractice suits and allegations of unethical conduct

- To identify the record as a resource that can help counselors face the challenges of accountability and ensure their ability to meet human needs

- To recognize everyday problems associated with ineffective communication, including how records can be used against counselors in a malpractice case or in an allegation of unethical behavior

- To demonstrate how records can be used to enhance the service relationship, promote consumer empowerment, and provide the counselor with a defense in the event of a lawsuit or allegation of unethical behavior
- To identify the record and the *ACA Code of Ethics* as resources that can help counselors face the challenges of accountability and ensure the ability to meet human needs
- To establish the *Code of Ethics* as a foundation for professional and personal behavior
- To increase overall understanding of professional values and principles of service
- To demonstrate how compliance with the *ACA Code* can reduce legal risk exposure
- To provide guidelines for resolution of ethical dilemmas

None of the editions of this monograph will provide a fail-safe solution to all record-keeping problems or every ethical dilemma. Certainly, the books are not a substitute for competent legal advice. Neither the American Counseling Association nor the author is liable for a reader's conduct or damages that may result from the use of training materials.

Forty-three years of experience, countless books, articles, consultations with associates, workshops I've attended, and the National Association of Social Worker's *Code of Ethics* aided in the development of my own workshops on documentation and ethical issues and this monograph. Although it is impossible to credit each source of information, this publication contains a list of references and suggested reading materials, some of which influenced the development of this work. When actual examples of clinical documentation are used, only names and dates have been changed to protect confidentiality.

You may not agree with everything in this monograph, and some material may not be applicable to your work. It is also important to understand that this monograph is about ethical conduct and risk management, not risk elimination. Nevertheless, the principles in this book are relevant to all social service and health care professionals, including those in mental health, developmental disability, substance abuse, schools, managed care, criminal justice, psychosocial rehabilitation, and case management, whether in private or public practice. Experienced staff will find this book a useful refresher course, and new staff will obtain a sound foundation upon which to base documentation and professional conduct.

Many of the essential elements of this monograph were developed in the live training workshops I have presented over the past two decades. This book cannot be as comprehensive or as much fun as a live workshop for several reasons. We are not in a room filled with people, and there is no opportunity for discussion. I cannot show my audiovisual tape (or DVD) titled *No Good Deed Will Go Unpunished.* In addition, in my workshops, I always have my guitar and sing a few songs. Today, we cannot sing together, but this monograph is written in the first person to maintain the feel of a live training program or workshop and permit you to more personally relate to the material and its presenter. I have even included the lyrics to some of the songs I sing at workshops in some of the chapters. Regardless, I hope to help you learn to write with pride as you document professional interventions and judgments. Finally, this monograph is designed not only to promote an understanding of and compliance with the *ACA Code of Ethics,* but also to reduce risk exposure related to unethical actions, malpractice lawsuits, and paybacks to funding sources.

Some of the information in this monograph is carried over from the first two editions because the principles of good record keeping and ethical conduct will always remain constant. Nevertheless, you will discover a significant amount of new information, especially as it relates to online counseling, cultural sensitivity, integrity, deception, misrepresentation, confidentiality, dual relationships, sexual relationships, ethical conduct, and steps for the resolution of ethical problems.

This monograph presupposes that you have a basic knowledge of your profession's code of ethics. If you have not reread it in the last year, do so now and keep a copy on your desk for ready reference. We will address the necessity for and an understanding of compliance with a code of ethics in order to deal more effectively with the numerous legal and moral complexities within society. Hopefully, the third edition will be a valuable tool to assist you in an era of increasing numbers of malpractice lawsuits, paybacks to funding sources, and allegations of unethical behavior.

As you read the following pages, you will note that the resource most frequently cited, of course, is the *ACA Code of Ethics*. I have attempted to correlate chapters to the specifics in the *Code*, so much so that pertinent *ACA Code* citations introduce most chapters. This monograph reinforces the purposes of the *ACA Code*, focusing specifically on the following goals outlined in the *Code's* Purpose:

- To establish "principles that define ethical behavior and best practices of association members"
- To serve as an "ethical guide designed to assist members in constructing a professional course of action that best serves those utilizing counseling services and best promotes the values of the counseling profession"
- To serve as the "basis for processing of ethical complaints and inquiries initiated against members of the association"

About the Author

ROBERT W. MITCHELL, ACSW, began his career as a children's protective service worker in 1959. Working on behalf of abused and neglected children, he made frequent court appearances and quickly learned the importance of good documentation and sound ethical judgment. He obtained a master's degree from the University of Louisville Raymond Kent School of Social Work in 1962.

In 1973, he was employed as a social worker by one of the largest mental health agencies in the nation. The organization was audited in 1978 and went bankrupt, in part because of its inadequate record keeping. It was an unpleasant but effective way to learn even more about the importance of documentation. Over the next 3 years Mr. Mitchell developed a training program designed to help counselors document professional judgments and interventions. His program, "What Every Clinician Should Know About Money," was published in 1981 in *Creativity and Innovation: Challenge of the 80s* (H. Fishman, Ed., pp. 117–126, Davis, CA: Pyramid).

He has been a member of the National Association of Social Workers since 1962 and the Academy of Certified Social Workers since 1965. The Kentucky Chapter of the National Association of Social Workers named Mr. Mitchell Social Worker of the Year in 1988. Later that year he also received the Distinguished Citizen Award from the mayor of Louisville and the Honorable Order of the Kentucky Colonels from the governor for services to the field of mental health.

In 1990, the National Association of Social Workers Malpractice Insurance Trust released *The Client Record and Professional Account-*

ability, an educational audiovisual tape based, in part, on his documentation and risk management workshop. The tape contains segments of his program and refers to him as an expert.

Mr. Mitchell was also a founding member of the American Association for Therapeutic Humor. Music has always been an extension of Mr. Mitchell's social work values, and the executive committee of the State Chapter of the National Association of Social Workers has proclaimed him the Kentucky Chapter Bard. His first recording, "I Need a Respite," was released in 1992. "Some Days This Place Is a Zoo" was released in 1994. The 1995 *Encyclopedia of Social Work* (19th ed., NASW Press) contains an article that notes Mr. Mitchell is one of a small number of professionals who commercially recorded music for a specific social-work–related purpose. According to the article, his "music evokes laughter and self-therapy for dealing with burnout." Several of his songs are included in this monograph.

In 1978, Mr. Mitchell moved from direct clinical service to finance and became the first manager of accounts receivable for Seven Counties Services, Inc., a mental health/developmental disability/substance abuse agency in Louisville, Kentucky. Later, he transferred to program planning and evaluation, and still later was promoted to internal compliance auditor for the $55 million organization.

He is a former member of the National Speakers Association and the Institute for Internal Auditors. As professional speaker, trainer, and author, Mr. Mitchell has provided training to over 250,000 professionals in 47 states and Canada. A partial listing of audiences includes the United States Psychiatric Rehabilitation Association (formerly the International Association of Psycho-Social Rehabilitation Services), the Canadian Mental Health Association, the Child Welfare League of America, the Mayo Clinic, the National Rehabilitation Association, the Mental Health in Corrections Symposium, the Association of Behavioral Healthcare Management, the American Association of Homes and Services for the Aging, the Alcohol and Drug Rehabilitation Wellness Institute, the National Association of Qualified Mental Retardation Professionals, the National Institute for Alternative Care Professionals, the American Professionals Society on Child Abuse and Prevention, the Developmental Disabilities Symposium, and 23 universities.

Since his retirement from Seven Counties Services, Inc., in December 2002, Mr. Mitchell has worked exclusively as an independent speaker and trainer, offering workshops from coast to coast.

Special Thanks

To my parents, Isabel and William Mitchell, for teaching me that if something is worth doing, it is worth doing well.

To my wife, Carolyn, for her encouragement to develop a workshop related to ethics and documentation as well as her love, patience, understanding, and support for 45 years.

To my children, Debbie and Rob, for their love and encouragement.

To Rita Gray Recktenwald for friendly but firm editing for the third time. She also edited the 1991 and 2001 editions of *Documentation in Counseling Records*. Her knowledgeable and sensitive contributions have created a more focused, more organized, and easier-to-use monograph. Her skillful assistance was central to the completion of this project, and I will always be grateful for her participation.

To the American Counseling Association for generous support and encouragement, and for the privilege of having published three books with the association, and especially to Director of Publications, Carolyn Baker, for her invaluable assistance with this monograph.

—*Robert W. Mitchell, ACSW*

Glossary

Client: The recipient of any professional intervention from a counselor. An individual seeking or referred to the professional services of a counselor for help with problem resolution or decision making. Also referred to as a consumer, patient, member, resident, or beneficiary. A client has also signed a form granting the counselor permission to provide service, or in the case of a child or person who has been declared incompetent, signed permission has been obtained from the parent/guardian, or the counselor has received a copy of a court order that provides a service directive.

Confidentiality: In general terms, the maintenance of client secrets, but the concept goes beyond the record and covers communication between counselor and client. The purpose of confidentiality is to encourage candor so that the client yields more thorough information, thereby promoting better diagnosis and treatment.

Counselor: A professional (or a student who is a counselor-in-training) engaged in a counseling practice or other counseling-related services. Counselors fulfill many roles and responsibilities such as counselor educators, researchers, supervisors, practitioners, and consultants.* The counselor is a service provider, and the term includes all professionals, including social workers, nurses, psychologists, psychiatrists, case managers, and therapists.

Culture: Membership in a socially constructed way of living, which incorporates collective values, beliefs, norms, boundaries, and

---

*Denotes verbatim definitions from the 2005 *ACA Code of Ethics* Glossary.

lifestyles that are cocreated with others who share similar worldviews comprising biological, psychosocial, historical, psychological, and other factors.*

Diversity: The similarities and differences that occur within and across cultures, and the intersection of cultural and social identities.*

Documents: Any written, digital, audio, visual, or artistic recording of the work within the counseling relationship between counselor and client.

Ethical conduct: The professional's actions, which must conform to the code of ethics developed and agreed to by other professionals in the field.

Multicultural/diversity competence: A capacity whereby counselors possess cultural and diversity awareness and knowledge about self and others, and how this awareness and knowledge is applied effectively in practice with clients and client groups.*

Multicultural/diversity counseling: Counseling that recognizes diversity and embraces approaches that support the worth, dignity, potential, and uniqueness of individuals within their historical, cultural, economic, political, and psychosocial contexts.*

Plan: A document that details why the client is being served and what is going to be done, and lists measurable and desired outcomes. Sometimes referred to as a treatment plan, individual habilitation plan, plan of care, service plan, residential plan, individual education plan, rehabilitation or vocational plan, or case management plan.

Privileged communication: The communication between a category of professionals and their clients, identified by state statute as privileged and not subject to disclosure. Privilege, like confidentiality in general, exists for the benefit of the client and can be waived by the client. There are many exceptions to general rules of law and ethics. When a judge orders a counselor to answer questions or to provide copies of the counseling record, the orders are absolute unless they are reversed by a higher court or suspended while a higher court is considering an appeal. As a result, counselors who comply with a judge's orders generally cannot be held liable even if someone's legal rights are violated in the process. Counselors who plan to refuse to comply must have their own attorney and must rely on legal advice. Counselors have an ethical responsibility to protest an order issued by a judge if they believe the order violates an ethical obligation. However, if a judge rules the order will stand, a counselor must comply or may be held in contempt of court.

Record: The organized file (paper or electronic) containing clinical, fiscal, demographic, and other information as deemed necessary for effective service delivery. Includes any information used for the purpose of diagnosis and treatment. The record is maintained in accordance with state standards, organizational procedure manuals, and funding source regulations. Also referred to as a chart or folder. May include any other written documents, audio or video recordings, or other tangible items that contain client information.

Service: A generic term referring to a professional intervention. Includes, but is not limited to, counseling, evaluation, consultation, individual therapy, family therapy, group therapy, art therapy, psychosocial rehabilitation, chemotherapy, behavior modification, case management, and home visits.

Staff note: A counselor's entry that documents professional judgment or intervention. Sometimes referred to as clinical entry, service note, progress note, daily note, group note, weekly summary, or service log.

Subpoena: A legal document issued under the auspices of a court, designed to compel a person to appear in court and give testimony. It may also require that the professional bring records to court.

Subpoena duces tecum: The legal document issued under the auspices of a court that requires submission of specific records as described in the subpoena.

CHAPTER 1

Ethical Behavior, Values, and Professional Standards

Professional values are an important way of living out an ethical commitment. Values inform principles. Inherently held values that guide our behaviors or exceed prescribed behaviors are deeply ingrained in the counselor and developed out of personal dedication, rather than the mandatory requirement of an external organization.
                              —*ACA Code of Ethics*, Preamble

ETHICAL CONDUCT

A person can run a red light every day, and the action has no public consequence until the driver hits or kills someone. Unethical conduct may be of no consequence (at least publicly) until an allegation is made or a malpractice lawsuit is filed. However, from the first moment of contact, you become responsible and accountable to your profession, the individuals you serve, your funding sources, your colleagues, the community, and a legal system that protects the rights of each individual.

As I began to develop an ethics workshop, I was struck by more than a dozen disconcerting news stories, all of which appeared in one week. Newspapers and TV broadcasts provided vivid examples of unethical conduct such as the following:

- Two young children starved to death as their mother lay in a drunken stupor. The home had been repeatedly investigated by the agency's professional staff, who concluded abuse and neglect allegations were unfounded.

- Medicaid audits located patients who were being prescribed drugs normally associated with conditions for which they had not been diagnosed or who were being prescribed unnecessary multiple drugs.
- A state circuit judge is charged with two counts of misconduct by the judicial conduct commission. He paid his wife for work she did not do and gave a female acquaintance special treatment on her felony case. His actions violated three canons of judicial conduct, including one requiring judges to avoid impropriety and the appearance of impropriety, and another requiring judges to perform duties impartially and diligently.

These are disturbing stories, but they are too common. The same week these stories appeared, the cartoon strip "Dilbert" was running a series related to ethics. Dilbert asks, "Is it immoral for my company to sell 40,000-calorie donuts?" The paraphrased reply was, "You're not forcing anyone to eat them. People cannot resist them even if they know the hazards. Free will is an illusion. People always choose the perceived path of greatest pleasure." That could be funny, if our topic were not so serious.

The people we serve are in difficult situations, and they are vulnerable. Therefore, we must elevate our involvement to the highest possible level. Our clients and our professions deserve nothing less.

The dictionary defines *ethical behavior* as conforming to accepted professional standards of conduct and a moral duty. A code of ethics, consequently, must be at the core of your professional and personal life. You are a professional, and the principles covered in this book are relevant regardless of your line of work and whether you are in a private or public setting.

It appears that not only professionals but also ordinary American citizens are aware of problems with integrity. In an article published in December 2005, the Associated Press reported that the word *integrity* topped an online dictionary's inquiries for definitions from seven million users and stated that this interest in the word reflects "the country's collective concern about its values." The article went on to quote journalism professor Ralph Whitehead, who said that the online interest "may indicate the continuing discussion about American values and morality, or perhaps that integrity itself is becoming scarce, so its definition is unfamiliar" ("'Integrity,'" 2005).

A code is designed to offer a set of values and standards to guide decision making and conduct. A code does not and cannot provide a set of rules that stipulate how you should act in every situation.

As the *ACA Code of Ethics* Purpose says, "When counselors are faced with ethical dilemmas that are difficult to resolve, they are expected to engage in a carefully considered ethical decision-making process. Reasonable differences of opinion can and do exist among counselors with respect to the ways in which values, ethical principles, and ethical standards would be applied when they conflict. While there is no specific ethical decision-making model that is most effective, counselors are expected to be familiar with a credible model of decision making that can bear public scrutiny and its application."

Reasonable differences of opinion will always exist, and the word *reasonable* is frequently used in discussions about ethical behavior. To clarify the term: when I speak of a reasonable person, I speak of a person who agrees with me. But seriously, one of the most difficult issues with any code is the use of words such as *reasonable, appropriate, adequate, responsible,* and *diligent*. Such words can and often do have different meanings for different people. There will always be an element of subjective opinion. That is why it is a difficult topic to address, but it is one that must be addressed if we are to be the best we can be.

A code cannot guarantee ethical behavior or resolve the complexity involved in making responsible choices. Rather, a code sets forth standards to which professionals aspire and by which their actions can be judged. Regardless of our profession, ethical behavior will result only from our personal commitment to engage in ethical practice.

Every code has multiple principles to which you should adhere. Three fundamental principles are service, competence, and confidentiality.

Service

A counselor's primary goal is to assist people in need. In so doing, it is essential that we respect the dignity of each client and elevate service to others above self-interest. The *Code* says, "Counselors are encouraged to contribute to society by devoting a portion of their professional activity to services for which there is little or no financial return (pro bono publico)" (A, Introduction).

Competence

Ethical counselors practice only within their areas of competence, and they keep their competence up to date through continuing education and professional development. The *Code* encourages counselors to participate in local, state, and national associations that foster the development and improvement of counseling skills. Don't forget to document your efforts and keep your personnel file current, because such documentation can be important in the event of an audit, a court appearance, a malpractice lawsuit, or allegations of unethical conduct. Implied in this standard is the need for a counselor to contribute to the knowledge base of his or her profession by presenting papers and workshops or offering supervision to the next generation of counselors. Also implied in this standard is the need to provide appropriate referral resources when requested or needed. The *Code* emphasizes the seriousness of competence so much that it states, "If counselors determine an inability to be of professional assistance to clients, they avoid entering or continuing counseling relationships" (A.11.b.).

Confidentiality

In general terms, this means the maintenance of personal, private client information, but in practice it goes beyond the record and covers communication between counselor and client. The purpose of confidentiality is to encourage candor so that the client yields more thorough information, thereby promoting better diagnosis and treatment.

Although we must make every reasonable effort to protect the confidentiality of all information obtained in the course of treatment, there may be compelling reasons for disclosure (e.g., to prevent serious, foreseeable, and imminent harm to a client or other identifiable persons). In such an instance, disclose the least amount of information necessary to achieve the desired purpose and, to the extent possible, inform clients about the disclosure and potential consequences before disclosure is made.

Discuss with clients and other interested parties the nature of confidentiality and its limitations by reviewing circumstances such as when information may be requested and when information may be legally required. Your discussion with the client should occur at the beginning of the therapeutic relationship, and reminders will be needed throughout the course of your involvement. Don't forget to document your discussions in the chart. As you read this monograph, you will see that the principle of confidentiality permeates all stages of the counselor–client interaction. Recognizing that "trust is a cornerstone of the counseling relationship," the *Code* cites the principles of confidentiality as a basic underpinning of ethical conduct (B, Introduction).

The *Code* offers directions for specific situations in which privacy is an issue:

- When services are provided to families, couples, or groups, obtain agreement among all of the parties involved concerning each individual's right to confidentiality and each individual's obligation to protect the information shared by others. Clients must be informed that counselors cannot guarantee that everyone will honor such an agreement. Again, don't forget to document your activity in the record. You may want to design a form for each person to sign.
- When information is disclosed to third-party payers, counselors obtain client authorization and then release only information pertinent to the request. You might also consider asking auditors to sign a form promising to respect the confidential information they read.
- When information is requested during a legal proceeding or when dealing with the press, the judicious counselor will work with an attorney who is familiar with appropriate state laws and understands the counselor's position and the code of ethics.

ENFORCEABLE AND ASPIRATIONAL GUIDELINES

In professional codes of any type, some standards are considered to be enforceable guidelines, and some are considered to be aspirational or strongly encouraged. The people who review alleged unethical conduct will use their best judgment in determining the extent to which each standard is enforceable. In other words, there will always be an element of subjectivity in discussions about ethics.

A code frequently employs the word *should*, a word the dictionary says is used to express a request in a polite manner or to suggest. The dictionary also contains stronger words: *shall* means mandatory, *must* means an imperative duty or requirement, and *will* expresses a command.

It is inevitable that individuals will not agree about what a code indicates must be done and what is strongly urged. Therefore, I suggest our professional and personal behavior be based on a belief that every standard is required. We have chosen a difficult profession in difficult times. With so much insensitivity and unprincipled behavior in our world, it is up to us to set the highest possible standard for excellence.

Depending on the counting method, there are 363 standards in the *ACA Code*. Another service provider's code may have more or fewer, but the issues addressed in this monograph are applicable to all helping professionals because our primary responsibility is to promote the well-being of clients. In general, clients' interests are primary. One aspect that makes the profession so difficult to work in is that your responsibility to the larger society or specific legal obligations may (on limited occasions) supersede the loyalty owed clients, and clients should be advised of this fact. The law, for example, requires you to report child abuse (and in some cases, elder abuse) and threats to harm self or others. Another complicating factor is a code's direction to respect and promote the right of clients to self-determination. However, there are occasions when a counselor may limit clients' rights when in his or her professional judgment, clients' actions or potential actions pose a serious risk to themselves or others.

The *Code* provides not only standards to which the general public can hold us accountable, but also standards that can be used to assess whether someone has engaged in unethical conduct. Alleged violations are subject to peer review, and the process is usually insulated from legal proceedings in order to permit a profession to discipline (or advise if necessary) its own members. The good news is that a violation of ethical standards does not automatically imply legal liability or violation of the law. The bad news is that, often, a final determination can be made only in the context of legal proceedings, which can be emotionally and financially draining. And, in these proceedings as in all legal proceedings, ignorance is no excuse. As the *ACA Code* clearly states, "Lack of knowledge or misunderstanding of an ethical responsibility is not a defense against a charge of unethical conduct" (H.1.a.). A counselor's best defense will always be a clear sense of ethical behavior and documentation to support that behavior.

Most professions have a formal procedure to review complaints filed against their members. If a complaint is filed against you, you are required to cooperate with the proceedings and to abide by any disciplinary rulings or sanctions.

Indeed, the *ACA Code* suggests lofty goals for professional counselors, including promoting change at all levels of society, improving the quality of life for individuals and groups, removing barriers to the provision and access to service, engaging in rigorous research, and maintaining their own emotional, physical, and mental health. This is hard work, but it is what we are about.

This monograph suggests that you get into the habit of turning to the *ACA Code of Ethics* for direction. No professional code is intended to sit on a bookshelf. Rather, a code is a living document designed to provide you with a solid foundation for your professional life.

My 40-plus years of experience have convinced me that most helping professionals are ethical and caring individuals who want to be of service to others. I believe the words to one of my songs describe the kind of people we all strive to be.

We Are a Gentle Caring People

A voice cries out, "Is anyone there?"
It is pleading, "Does anyone care?"
A world can be lonely and so very sad.
The people we see, they feel so bad.
Does anybody care?

Couples are homeless and have no place to sleep.
In sadness they weep, their depression is so deep.
Families are broken when parents divorce.
There will be pain for the children, of course.
Does anybody care?

The kids in school cannot concentrate.
Without some support, you can guess their fate.
They want a job but they have no skill.
They need some training. Their fight is uphill.
Does anybody care?

Folks will complain, "All that funding is in vain!"
And our efforts are disdained.
Still we give our all day after day,
trying to make blue skies from gray.
Oh, yes, somebody cares!
We are a gentle caring people
and we're helping, helping every day.

A Legal Perspective

Counselors maintain records necessary for rendering professional services to their clients and as required by laws, regulations, or agency or institution procedures. Counselors include sufficient and timely documentation in their client records to facilitate the delivery and continuity of needed services. Counselors take reasonable steps to ensure that documentation in records accurately reflects client progress and services provided. If errors are made in client records, counselors take steps to properly note the correction of such errors according to agency or institutional policies.
—ACA Code of Ethics, A.1.b.

My professional career began in 1959 as a child protective service caseworker, so I was in a juvenile courtroom working with attorneys my first week on the job. It did not take long for me to discover that inadequate documentation can be used effectively against a counselor and his or her agency. In the intervening years, I have learned a great deal about an attorney's perspective on the issues that are discussed in this monograph. An awareness of that perspective is an invaluable asset for any counseling professional.

Remember, attorneys have an obligation to advocate their clients' interest to the best of their ability. If you find yourself facing a malpractice suit or an allegation of unethical conduct, someone has told his or her lawyer that you are incompetent, that your programs are ineffective, or that your conduct was unethical. Some of the most frequent reasons for court appearances relate to breach of confidentiality, suicide, attempted suicide, violent behavior, sexual involvement, failure to provide a safe environment, incorrect treatment, improper placement, failure to be available when needed, and negligence in hiring and supervising staff. This chapter and subsequent chapters explain how these issues, your documentation, and your conduct are related to a code of ethics.

CREDENTIALS

A clear, verifiable record of credentials must be maintained for every professional. The individual, not an employer, is responsible for maintaining his or her own file and making it readily available for hiring purposes or for any legal or ethical issue that may arise.

If you are in a position to hire staff and they say they are a certified counselor, registered nurse, certified psychologist, licensed social worker, or other professional, unfortunately you cannot take their word for it. You must obtain a copy of their current license or certification. Many times individuals fail to renew their certifications, and some do not complete their studies. Obtain a copy of a valid transcript or diploma and place it in the individual's human resources file. You must also check references, former employers, and perhaps consider a criminal background check (which may be required). It is also important to keep copies of this information in the individual's personnel file.

On a related matter, it is your responsibility to maintain your own personnel file. It must always be current and comprehensive. For example, each time you participate in a training program, document the date, the length, the topic, the name and credentials of the instructor, and information about whether the course qualifies for CEUs.

Client charts and personnel files are of use to a plaintiff's attorney only in so far as they help establish a reasonable doubt about your competence, the quality of your interventions, or your conduct. Even if a claim against you is invalid, you must defend yourself, and inadequate documentation in the counseling chart and personnel file could result in damage to your professional reputation.

CHARTING ESSENTIALS

Documentation is a key element underpinning many directives in the *Code*. Especially pertinent are those areas in the chart that must be documented:

- Integrated counseling plans that offer reasonable promise of success and are consistent with clients' abilities and circumstances
- Written reviews of the rights and responsibilities of both the counselor and client
- Documented discussions of informed consent throughout the counseling relationship
- Information provided to clients about issues such as, but not limited to, goals, procedures, and potential risks and benefits of services
- Documentation of the counselor's qualifications, credentials, and experience
- Explanations of any counselor–client nonprofessional interaction and the rationale for such interaction

The *Code,* as well as basic good practice, requires clear and understandable language in all documentation. This is easy to say but hard to do. A substantial part of the first and second editions of this monograph discussed in detail guidelines for effective language in counseling records: language that is readable, accurate, sufficient, timely, relevant, and respectful of the client. Additional discussion of some techniques for such writing will be found in this and subsequent chapters.

Throughout this monograph, selected news stories from 47 states (a small sampling from hundreds of such stories) are shared to emphasize the relevance of documentation and ethical conduct. Names of states, organizations, and individuals have been deleted to ensure confidentiality. The *Code,* for example, stipulates that documentation in records must accurately reflect the services provided. Newspaper headlines such as "Child welfare employee charged with falsifying records in case of slain boy" indicate that such a stipulation is not always met.

As you read the following actual examples reported in news articles, ask yourself what ethical standards have been violated:

- Deaths of four emaciated children show flaws in child protection system. Suffering went unseen in a home that looked loving.
- Deaths of mentally retarded clients spur investigation and lawsuit. Group home offered little oversight.

- Patients in assisted living facilities require closer supervision. Investigations discovered injuries, sexual assault, neglect, and medication errors.
- Patients engaging in sexual conduct and subdued through excessive use of restraints and medication to control behavior. The client's mother told a reporter, "I thought this was a safe place to take my child to get help, but it ended up hurting him more than helping him."
- Patient chokes on his own vomit, possibly from a drug overdose.
- Child welfare agency employees found to have criminal records for child abuse, grand theft, DUI manslaughter, drugs, aggravated assault with a weapon, and welfare fraud.

TESTIMONY AND DOCUMENTATION

The ability to analyze and understand the reasons for these kinds of violations is essential for all human services professionals. It becomes critical when a professional is summoned to court to testify. Although lawsuits against counselors have been increasing each year, statistics indicate that most counselors will not be sued or charged with unethical conduct. Nevertheless, there is a high likelihood that you or your records will, at some time, be in a courtroom. The legal system believes you and/or your client charts may have information needed to make an informed decision in a child custody dispute, an involuntary hospitalization, and a wide array of other situations. Here are some suggestions that may be useful in the event you are ordered to appear before the court or submit a record:

- *In court:* Tell the truth. A lie can lose the case, no matter how small or unimportant the falsehood may seem. Be sure to discuss the case truthfully with your attorney before you get on the stand.
  In charting: Write the truth. Words must be an accurate reflection of the situation, precise and current. Horace Mann said, "You need not tell all the truth, unless to those who have a right to know. But let all you tell be the truth."
- *In court:* Do not guess. If you do not know or cannot remember, say so.

In charting: Do not make assumptions. If you suspect something, your opinion must be substantiated. If you do not know something or cannot remember, do not write it.

- *In court:* Be sure you understand the question before you answer. When in doubt, ask the attorney to explain or to use language you understand. You cannot provide a truthful or accurate answer unless you understand the question.

  In charting: Understand the purpose of the counseling record. If a judgment or intervention is not documented, it was not rendered. Effective communication requires a mutually understandable vocabulary. Write in words that you or another will understand.

- *In court:* Take your time. Be certain that you are answering the question being asked; then respond. If the question is complicated, wait for your attorney to offer an objection. Then wait for the judge to make a ruling. You may not have to answer every question.

  In charting: Take your time. Be certain you understand the importance of the charting. Include information that is logical and relates to the plan of care. Do not rush; you may inadvertently neglect to include clinically relevant data.

- *In court:* Answer only the question that is asked and stop. An attorney will ask for additional information when it is needed. You could inadvertently provide too much information and break a confidence.

  In charting: Enter only information which is pertinent to the client's situation and stop. The counseling record should be a logical, short story. It begins with an assessment and moves to a plan, staff notes, case reviews, and a termination. Generally speaking, if an entry does not relate to the problems listed in the most recent plan or review, it is not necessary. I am reminded of a story of the small child who came home and asked, "Where did I come from?" The nervous parents then went into a detailed explanation of where babies come from. "No, No!" the horrified child shouted when the explanation was through. "Jimmy comes from Kentucky! Where do I come from?" In short, answer the question asked and nothing more.

- *In court:* Talk loudly enough to be heard. Sit erect, do not chew gum, and keep your hands away from your mouth.

  In charting: Write legibly and organize your thoughts before you write them. Eliminate unfounded opinions and maintain a current record.

- *In court:* Enunciate and give clear answers so the court reporter can record accurate exchanges. An answer is not a nod of the head or a shrug of the shoulders.

  In charting: Use easily understood words; define the terms because professional jargon may not always mean the same thing to everyone; eliminate qualifiers as often as possible.

- *In court:* Be aware of questions involving time. When you are making an estimate or expressing an opinion, let the court know it is your estimate or opinion.

  In charting: Be specific about dates (include month, day, and year). When you are making an estimate or expressing an opinion, label the entry *clinical opinion* or *diagnostic impression.*

- *In court:* Be calm. There is often a tendency to become hostile or defensive. Anger and hostility will distract the judge and jury from what you have to say. During the preparation of this monograph, one newspaper article detailed the story of a professional who was jailed for "tone, attitude, and contemptuous behavior." The professional, however, claimed to be "acting as a child advocate." Obviously, the situation was more complex than briefly described here. Nevertheless, a professional's courtroom demeanor influenced a judge.

  In charting: Be calm. When you become frustrated with a client, office situation, or a family member, an entry can reflect those negative feelings and distract from the clinical information. A staff note can say more about the writer than the client. I am reminded of a note that said, "John was more cooperative than expected." Another note said, "Jane's next appointment is August 22nd. I'll bet she does not keep it." That kind of entry tells a reader something about the writer but not much about the patient.

- *In court:* Be courteous. Say, "Yes sir/madam" or "No sir/madam." Address the judge as "Your Honor."

In charting: Be courteous. Words can be mean spirited. I have actually found the following words in client charts: *obnoxious, fat, stupid, lazy,* and *stubborn.* Define adjectives; use words that specifically describe behaviors. Involve the client as often as possible in the documentation process. It is courteous and can be an effective part of the treatment process. It also promotes empowerment.

- *In court:* Looks are important. A professional's appearance is almost as important as the substance of his or her remarks.

  In charting: Looks are also important. Records must reflect the professional you are. Charts must be current, logical, legible, neat, and organized. Blank spaces, out-of-sequence notes, sloppiness, and altered information will have a negative impact on credibility.

- *In court:* Give a definite answer when you can. There is a tendency to hesitate in response to a question such as, "Are you absolutely sure?" If you are certain, be firm and do not be afraid to say so.

  In charting: Write with pride and professional authority. Remember, too, that usefulness requires specificity, and vague writing could be interpreted as incompetence. Records should not be filled with a preponderance of qualifiers such as *seems, appears,* and *possibly.* Use these words sparingly.

- *In court:* Trial preparation is proper and necessary.

  In charting: Think before you write. It is often difficult or impossible to take back what you have documented. Do not forget, others may need the chart when you are not available, so write in a style that will be understood by you or a coworker. Reportedly, many people had difficulty understanding the work of poet Robert Browning. Playwright Rudolf Besier, in his play *The Barrets of Wimpole Street,* recounts an incident with Browning's ardent admirer and soon-to-be wife, poet Elizabeth Barrett. She is said to have asked him to explain one of his poems, and after he re-read it, he said, "When I wrote that, God and I knew what it meant. Today, only God knows." If you or I read your notes 6 weeks from now, will we know what you meant?

Your competence and integrity as a professional are demonstrated through complete and understandable documentation. Periodic review of your own documentation techniques will help ensure that any deficiencies are corrected.

MISSING AND INCOMPLETE ENTRIES

One of the most frequent record-keeping deficiencies is missing entries. You can complain about paperwork, but if you have no documentation, you have no defense. A lawyer once told me in jest that one of the first things he was taught in law school was, "In God we trust; all others must document."

Another common problem in the counseling record relates to missing, incomplete, or altered dates. Be sure each entry lists month, day, and year. Do not leave anything out, or you create doubt.

Incomplete forms and blank spaces provide a lawyer with an opportunity to walk over to the jury, show them your half-completed work, and suggest you were not competent enough to obtain the information, or you did not care enough to obtain it. These statements may not be true, but the fact that someone did not complete the form provides an attorney with an opportunity to generate doubt about a counselor's ability. Maybe the information did not apply, but how are other readers supposed to know that if you do not tell them? When something does not apply, write *not applicable* in the space.

Sign each entry with your name, not initials. Then list your credentials (e.g., certified counselor, licensed social worker, registered nurse). Many counselors sign their name and list a job title, but that is not as effective as listing your credentials because not everyone understands or agrees about the difference between a Counselor I and a Counselor IV or a Therapist and a Senior Therapist. In this age of electronic records, a signature is still important. You will need a system that ensures that the signature on the screen (or a hard copy) confirms that that individual is the one who made the entry and that the note has not been altered.

ALTERED DOCUMENTATION

One of a lawyer's best friends is an altered document. If you make a mistake, the most universally acceptable method to make a correction is to use a pen and draw a line through the entry. But never obliterate words; they must remain legible. Above the line write the word *error* and, hopefully, on the same page, write the words *corrected entry*; then enter the correct information. If you discover an error several weeks after the entry has been made, draw a line through the entry (never obliterate words; they must be legible). Above the line write the word *error*, enter the date of the change, and initial it. Then, hopefully, on the same page, write the words *corrected entry*, enter the correct information, and cross-reference it with the original note.

If you delete one or two words from a sentence, the meaning of a sentence can be changed, and yet I have read records with five or six lines deleted. That sort of thing allows an attorney to walk over to the jury, show them your altered document, and say, "I wonder what the provider is trying to hide?" Maybe nothing, but you altered a document, didn't you?

THE RECORD AS LEGAL DEFENSE

With a court order, a lawyer can get a great deal of your chart. Maybe not everything, but enough to help establish doubt, and maybe, guilt. Is the record going to help *you* or a lawyer who is looking for inadequate, vague, or conflicting information or evidence of unethical conduct? There are more lawsuits and allegations of unethical behavior than ever before, so it is not surprising that there are also expanding theories of liability.

As a professional counselor, you will constantly deal with three conflicting principles:

1. The client's right of confidentiality versus the counselor's obligation to protect society
2. The client's right to receive service in the least restrictive setting versus the counselor's obligation to provide close supervision, continuous monitoring, and a safe environment
3. The client's right to die versus the counselor's obligation to save lives

When a client is suicidal, you may wish to involve the family, because if there is a suicide, surviving family members can sue you. An attorney will attempt to show that the counselor did not properly supervise the client, provide a safe environment, or was not qualified.

The mere fact that you exercised what you considered good judgment will not protect you. Someone once told me, "The truth is irrelevant; it is the evidence that counts." One counselor's attorney said, "I would rather have a good chart than anything else."

EIGHT WAYS TO GUARANTEE A LAWSUIT OR ALLEGATIONS OF UNETHICAL CONDUCT

There are eight sure ways to guarantee that a lawsuit or allegations of unethical conduct could be brought against you:

1. Document that something needs to be done; then do not do it.
2. Do not keep records current.
3. Do not obtain complete assessments or develop a comprehensive treatment plan.
4. Establish policies and procedures, but do not follow them.
5. Do not review or audit your records.
6. Nurture a dependent relationship and then cut it off abruptly.
7. Combine a suicidal client with a provider who has a reputation for sexual impropriety.
8. Ignore your code of ethics.

This chapter is not designed to intimidate or frighten you but rather to prepare you for the possibility of legal action or allegations of unethical conduct, however slight. But it is highly likely that you and/or your records may be brought into court to provide testimony in custody disputes, placement decisions, and a wide array of other situations. Being prepared for these types of situations is every professional's responsibility. If you are not prepared for the unexpected, then you will not be prepared for the consequences.

CHAPTER 3

A Fiscal Perspective

Counselors are accurate, honest, and objective in reporting their professional activities and judgments to appropriate third parties, including courts, health insurance companies, those who are the recipients of evaluation reports, and others.
—*ACA Code of Ethics*, C.6.b.

Some counselors rely on third-party funding for a portion of their operating revenue. It might be a special grant, designated state funding, Medicaid, Medicare, or any other insurance company. When you accept funding, you must also accept the payer's regulations. Auditors who monitor health care and social service organizations read counseling records to determine the validity of billings. When documentation is missing or considered insufficient, a payback will be requested and future funding may be placed in jeopardy. This chapter focuses, therefore, on what an auditor looks for in the review process.

The first thing an auditor looks for is a plan of care. It may also be titled treatment plan, habilitation plan, family plan, or service plan. Simply put, the auditor will look for a document that verifies the need for the service. If there is no need, the payer has no obligation to pay you.

The second thing an auditor will read is the staff note. The substance of counseling entries must verify a legally reimbursable service as the funding source defines it. If you are not sure what to write, obtain a copy of the payer service definitions and study them.

Then, use some of their words because they may not understand your professional terminology. More importantly, if you are not providing services as they define them, stop billing because it is illegal and unethical. Payers have not only specific definitions for a payable service or reimbursable activity but also specific regulations regarding educational qualifications for anyone who bills them. Additionally, some interventions are never payable, so it is important to contact the third-party payer before billing starts. It is the counselor's ethical responsibility to verify with the payer which providers and methodologies are reimbursable.

When a third party is billed, it is important to remember the golden rule: those who have the gold make the rules and can change the rules when they want. It is your responsibility to know what the funding source requires and what the code of ethics prescribes. It is incumbent upon the counselor to establish and maintain billing practices that accurately reflect the nature and extent of services provided and that identify who provided the service.

Accurate records ensure compliance with a code of ethics and can also ensure cash flow. Consider the following news item and information from the Medicare Web site:

- "Agency must repay state $2 million in Medicaid." Why? The organization billed for "therapy," but staff notes verified exercise class, parties, and field trips to parks, bowling alleys, and shopping malls. Unqualified staff also provided services.
- Several years ago, the Medicare Web site contained an article that stated, in part, "The inspector general audit found services to be inappropriate, rendered by unqualified staff, undocumented, or poorly documented (canned language appeared to be computer generated) . . . services were unnecessary because the recipient lacked the cognitive or communication skills necessary to participate in and benefit from therapy."

Managed care companies also require plans and notes to justify medical or psychiatric necessity. Most importantly, a counselor must acknowledge the fact that the managed care company makes all final decisions about what is reasonable and necessary. The content of your record must demonstrate benefits and outcome measures. One managed care company brochure contains the following warning: "To avoid patient malingering, two audits per year will be conducted."

Counselors frequently ask for the magic words that will ensure satisfactory records. Unfortunately, there is no set of words that assures acceptance from every auditor. Nevertheless, common sense and good practice can help address such concerns. The next section offers some more specific guidelines.

WHAT NOT TO DO

- Do not write a plan that ignores the problems listed in the assessment.
- Do not write a review that ignores the problems listed in the most recent notes.
- Do not write a plan that fails to verify team collaboration.
- Do not use "witty" group names to indicate reimbursable or professional therapy. Names such as "Personality Plus," "Men in Black," or "Over-the-Hill Gang" (actual titles that have appeared in records I have read) are not likely to verify the rendering of a payable service in the mind of an auditor.
- Do not write group notes that focus on a social activity rather than a professional intervention. Unless you can document how the activity was used to facilitate a therapeutic service, avoid writing about playing cards, making cookies, celebrating a birthday, bowling, or taking a trip.
- Do not write notes that are an observation or opinion only.
- Do not write that a client "benefited" or "enjoyed self" if there is no verification of the counseling service or the therapeutic benefit.
- Do not write notes that are brief or vague, making it difficult to determine the specific type of service or how the session related to the goals listed in the plan.

WHAT YOU MUST DO

You must maintain a record that is legible and current, and an accurate description of rendered services. After the client assessment has been obtained, you must develop a plan of care.

The *ACA Code* provides an additional directive: "When client treatment involves a continued review or participation by a treatment team, the client will be informed of the team's existence and composition, information being shared, and the purposes of sharing such information" (B.3.b.).

The components of a plan of care will include but are not limited to five items:

1. *Problem statement:* What are the specific problems? An unclear example is "anxiety." To make it clear, write something like "anxiety related to possible loss of job."

2. *Goal statement and expected date of goal achievement:* What specifics will result from counseling? Set specific and measurable goals that relate to the specific problems listed in the assessment. If you can see a specific behavior related to the problem or if you hear the client say something related to the problem, then the goal is more likely to be acceptable to an auditor. If you write a goal such as "Become responsible and maintain remission," ask the clients to repeat it like this, "Watch me become responsible and maintain remission." Then write "Take medications as prescribed" or "Remain in community for 6 months without readmission to hospital."

3. *Treatment modality:* Information in the assessment must confirm a need for the kind of service listed in this section of the plan. An unclear example of the service to be provided is "non-threatening support." A clear example might be "weekly group therapy for depressed men." To be a billable service, a covered professional who is considered qualified by the funding source must provide the intervention. The *Code* requires that, "Counselors practice only within the boundaries of their competence" (C.2.a.). So an ethical counselor must ask himself or herself, "Am I authorized and qualified to provide the treatment(s) listed in a plan of care?" If the answer is no, a counselor should arrange for the client to be seen by someone who is qualified. Counselors must also ask themselves if the listed modality is a reimbursable activity. As the *Code* clarifies, "Counselors practice in specialty areas new to them only after appropriate education, training, and supervised experience" (C.2.b.).

4. *Clinical impression or diagnosis:* The *Code* cautions counselors to "take special care to provide proper diagnosis of mental disorders" (E.5.a.). The diagnosis must be an accurate and unprejudiced reflection of the patient's mental health as indicated in the plan and in the assessment. Spell out the full diagnostic terms and list the complete *Diagnostic and Statistical Manual of Mental Disorders* (*DSM-IV-TR;* American Psychiatric Association, 2000) codes or *The International Classification of Mental and Behavioral Disorders: Clinical Descriptions and Diagnosis Guidelines* (*ICD-10;* World Health Organization, 2003) codes. Some diagnostic codes are not reimbursable. Do not overstate a client's condition to make it appear as though the individual has a billable diagnosis. To do so is illegal and unethical.

5. *Names and credentials:* Names and credentials of each person who participated in the development of the plan as well as the name of the assigned therapist must be listed. The person who wrote the plan or review must sign and date it. In many cases, the MD must also sign. Any individual who did not actually participate in the formulation of a plan should not sign or have his or her name listed. The *Code* emphasizes the importance of appropriate state and national professional credentials, and appropriate professional experience.

The best-organized plan, one incorporating these five components, must still be current and dynamic to demonstrate the need for reimbursable service and continuity of care.

ESSENTIAL ELEMENTS FOR THE STAFF NOTE

Once a plan of care has been clearly set up, staff notes document that the specific services listed in the plan have been provided. The notes, of course, must also be precise and should contain the following essential elements:

1. *Confirmation of a service:* Verbs are important. What did you do? What did the patient do? Use action words such as *focused, stabilized, recommended, discussed, assisted, advised, identified, assessed, referred, medicated, evaluated,* or *interpreted.* Verbs not only help auditors understand what was done but also help a coworker who needs information when you are not available.

2. *Verification of the information implied within a billing code:* Will the content of a staff note confirm (a) the same date as the billed date, (b) the same number of billed minutes (units of service), (c) the same kind of professional, and (d) the same type of service? If a billing code indicates a certified counselor provided a 45-minute individual therapy session on August 22, 2009, can you imagine the fiscal implications of a note dated, instead, August 27, 2009, titled "group therapy for 30 minutes" and signed by a case manager? As an auditor, I have seen such discrepancies.

3. *An original, legible signature, not a rubberstamp or initials:* Some notes must also be cosigned. The only way to know what a funding source requires is to read and comply with your state's licensure and funding source regulations.

Good staff notes connect interventions to the plan. Nouns are important. What issues received your professional intervention? Use words such as *aggression, anxiety, depression, hostility, isolation, medication, dependence,* or *rationalization.* A counselor must read the payer service definitions because some terms used in a staff note may not confirm a reimbursable service (e.g., *education, socialization, encouragement, religion, art,* or *music*).

Each person is capable of a multitude of mannerisms for any given characteristic. When you use words such as *abusive, argumentative,* or *dangerous,* you must define them or list the specific behavior or client statement. Other words that cause confusion are *demanding, disturbed, resistive, spontaneous, regressed, evasive, indifferent, unresponsive, disruptive, compulsive, extensive, impaired,* or *psychotic.* Frequently used conclusionary terms (unfounded, unsubstantiated opinions) include *delusional, violent, argumentative, unfit, abusive, dependent, immature, uncooperative, unrealistic, demanding, manipulative, dysfunctional family, sexual psychopath,* or *heavy drinker.* If these are the issues you deal with, write about them. But explain them in the context of the service provided and define them with phrases like "as evidenced by" or "as indicated by" (for more information, see chapter 5).

The best humorous advice I have found on the topic of documentation is this: "Writing is easy; all you do is sit staring at a blank sheet of paper until the drops of blood form on your forehead," and "Just leave out the words that will get you in trouble."

GUIDELINES FOR ETHICAL BILLING

As I hope this chapter has indicated, nowhere is precision in word choice more important for the professional counselor than in writing the plan of care and the notes that support it. Here are some other guidelines to keep in mind:

- Never bill for a service you did not provide. Never embellish or lie in a note for the purpose of making it appear that a billable service was rendered. The note must be an accurate reflection of the service you provided. You are a professional, and as such, your actions must be legal, moral, and ethical. Any deviation is unacceptable.
- Do not provide a 40-minute service and bill for 1 hour, unless you have an authorized procedure explaining when billed time is rounded up or rounded down. List start and stop times on each entry.
- Services provided by a counselor or social worker should not be billed as a service provided by a psychiatrist in order to obtain a higher rate of reimbursement.

Professional activity alone is never reason enough to expect payment for a service. When you are in your office writing a plan or staff note, imagine that you are actually signing your own paycheck. Why? Because when an auditor reviews your documentation and concludes that your content does not verify the rendering of a reimbursable service by a qualified provider to an eligible client, you and/or your agency will not be paid or may even be asked to make a refund of monies already received. More than one agency has been denied payment or gone bankrupt for just this reason.

CHAPTER 4

A Coworker's Perspective

Counselors maintain records necessary for rendering professional services to their clients and . . . include sufficient and timely documentation in their client records to facilitate the delivery and continuity of needed services. Counselors take reasonable steps to ensure that documentation in records accurately reflects client progress and services provided.

—*ACA Code of Ethics, A.1.b.*

Counselors have a special obligation to maintain clear records for their working colleagues to ensure continuity of care for their clients. Too often, it is the coworker who is put in a difficult position of trying to understand an inaccurate or incomplete record that he or she did not write, but must read and act upon. This chapter assumes the voice of that coworker.

You and I work together for the same agency. We have met casually, but we don't know each other well and have not had an opportunity to work together. Today you are out sick, and there is an emergency with one of your cases. I am on call and must see your client "Judie." Since you are not here, I retrieve the record and head for the appointment with your client. Is the chart legible? Current? Will I ask the same questions you've already asked? Will I be able to continue your clinical work effectively? I must rely entirely on your written record to answer these questions and serve the client well.

CONCLUSIONARY TERMS, MODIFIERS, AND ABBREVIATIONS

One note says, "Judie is unable to interact appropriately with others." What was the behavior? Who are the "others"? What did you do, and how did she respond? Our receptionist told me you saw her seven times, but there are only four notes. It is essential that I know what happened in those other three sessions. When entries are vague observations, I am uncertain as to the clinical significance.

Since the assessment and plan contain *conclusionary terms*, that is, modifiers without explanation, I am unsure what you meant when you wrote, "She is aggressive, intentionally destructive, and low functioning." I cannot imagine what would happen to relationships with clients who read their records only to learn they are viewed as immature, disorganized, combative, defiant, belligerent, unmotivated, inadequate, or explosive. Nevertheless, these words appear in Judie's chart without clarification.

When we document behavior, we need to choose modifiers carefully. Adjectives and adverbs can equate to unsubstantiated opinions. When you use words such as *delusional, violent, unfit, abusive, dependent,* or *uncooperative,* defining the term by adding "as evidenced by" or "as indicated by" will help make the record understandable. Opinions can make a powerful entry and verify the fact that we are professionals. Opinions, however, should be clearly acknowledged as such, and their sources indicated.

As I continue reading Judie's chart, several entries contain abbreviations that cause confusion. Does *ARC* mean American Red Cross? Alcohol Rehabilitation Center? Association for Retarded Citizens? Admission and Release Committee? Acute Residential Care? Or Aids Related Complex? Does *CD* mean chemical dependency or cognitive disorder? I need to know. The use of abbreviations can save us time, but it is important for everyone within our organization to use the same abbreviations to mean the same things. If the record is to be an effective tool for communication, there must be a mutually understandable vocabulary. Perhaps there are some internal guidelines somewhere, but I am not aware of them.

PROBLEMATIC STAFF NOTES

I also encountered your staff note describing Judie as nonverbal, but that was contradicted by sentences such as, "The client and I talked about the letter she left at the office"; "The client and I talked about ways she could deal with negative feelings she has about herself"; and "The client and I talked about her relationship with others and her daily activities." What "ways" were discussed? What "negative feelings" does this client have? Again, further defining the adjective *negative* would be helpful. I am also wondering, What "relationships"? What "daily activities"?

Another note says, "I praised Judie for her honesty and trust in me." Is this clinically significant? One of the most frequent complaints I have heard from record reviewers is that when they read a plan and the subsequent notes, they don't know they are reading about the same person. Before we write anything, we might ask ourselves, "Does this sentence have anything to do with the problem that brought the client here? Does it relate to the goals and objectives listed in the most recent plan of care or case review?" I'm not clear about how this statement relates.

Yet another note says, "It seems the client wrote a letter out of depression with possible suicidal ideation present." The word *seems* causes doubt. As often as possible, it helps to eliminate words like *seems* or *appears* to lessen doubt and increase confidence in the record. I need more specific information about her "suicidal ideation." The note also says she "seems satisfied with herself." This too causes confusion because Judie has been described as depressed and possibly suicidal. You could eliminate the confusion by asking a question and using Judie's own words (e.g., "I will not hurt myself. In fact, I haven't felt as comfortable around people in a long time. I'm not as lonely and depressed as I was 6 months ago."). Using the client's words eliminates doubt and may also document progress in dealing with problems.

The note also said, "Judie seems satisfied with present activities but concluded she would like to become more involved in arts and crafts, as she is extremely talented." Again, the word *seems* causes this entry to lose its clinical usefulness. What significance is there in satisfaction or lack of it? If this kind of information relates to a plan, specifying the nature of that relationship would help clarify the meaning. Who said she is "extremely talented"? Is this Judie's opinion of herself and is the information significant?

Still further, the note said, "Client seemed to be much more relaxed and seemed to smile easily." Does this have anything to do with the plan of care? If it does, it should be elaborated on in the note with greater specificity. Frequent use of qualifiers might cause someone to wonder about the competence of the provider to make clinical observations and draw appropriate conclusions for the direction of subsequent services. We certainly will never be able to completely eliminate the use of qualifiers, but we should use them sparingly.

POSSIBLE REPERCUSSIONS

The more I read, the more uneasy I become. Your staff note indicates you will "set up an appointment as soon as possible" but no date or time was scheduled, and today I am seeing this client with little to assist me. What could possibly happen because I have incomplete and confusing information?

- I could make an inappropriate referral.
- I could inadvertently break a confidence.
- I could alienate Judie and her family if they are dissatisfied with my intervention.
- Judie or someone in the family could contact a lawyer to initiate legal action on the grounds of incompetence or unethical conduct.
- Judie or someone in the family could contact a professional licensure board to initiate a formal complaint of incompetence or unethical conduct.

I know, colleague, that you did not intentionally provide a problematic record. But you are the only one who has first-hand knowledge about this client: what the problems are, what is being done to help her, and what needs to be done in the future. I wish you were here to help me make sure I understand your documentation, so I can do justice to your work and meet the client's needs.

Thus concludes our coworker's complaint, which would be tough to hear for any professional about a record he or she wrote. But to be fair, it is a legitimate complaint and concern. Counselors must understand that others rely on their documentation when they are not available. Both primary counselor and coworker are concerned about every client's welfare, and they must work together.

CLEAR, ACCURATE STAFF NOTES

No matter what stage of the counseling process you are in, in order to provide a useful and clear record for your associates, there are certain basic operating principles to which you should adhere. Here are five important ones:

1. Choice of language should be clear and specific. Avoid irrelevant statements. Eliminate excess words when possible. Instead of writing, "The client does not have any brothers or sisters," write "No siblings."

2. To eliminate or reduce doubt, use the client's own words. Quotations will provide a better picture of the individual's thoughts and feelings. Good writing is said to be 80 to 90% good listening. Write it as you hear it. A reasonable and defensible quote is usually two sentences or less.

3. After an entry has been made in the chart, ask yourself this question, "Am I comfortable sharing with the client what I have written, or reading it in the newspaper?"

4. Records must be a logical sequence of events. Before the counselor writes anything, he or she should ask, "Does this sentence have anything to do with the problem that brought the client here? Does it relate to the goals and objectives listed in the most recent plan of care or case review?" If yes, write it. If no, evaluate relevance. When information is not pertinent to provided services, there is no need to include it. If information is relevant, however, include it and be specific. Usefulness requires specificity, and vague writing might be construed as indicating incompetence.

5. Abstract phrases cause confusion and doubt. Enter a specific date rather than writing "soon," "someday," "in the near future," or "within a few days." Someone sent me a memo that said, "Staff assigned the vehicular spaces in the area adjacent to

our building are hereby informed that such utilization will be temporarily suspended on Monday of this week only." It should have said, "No parking allowed on Monday."

By now, you may be feeling some frustration and believe you cannot write an entry that will satisfy everyone. The fact is that you will never be able to write the perfect entry that will satisfy everyone. However, with some effort, you can establish and maintain a record that is understandable and accountable, and that will serve both your client and your coworkers' needs.

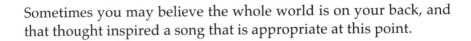

Sometimes you may believe the whole world is on your back, and that thought inspired a song that is appropriate at this point.

We've Got the Whole World on Our Back

This job of mine sure is fun.
At the end of a day I'm never done.
The real problem is, my brain's gone numb.
The whole world's on our back.

I serve people every day 'til I can't think straight.
I'm always outnumbered; that's my fate.
And don't you know it—I'm lawsuit bait!
The whole world's on our back.

Those friendly auditors are coming next week.
If they find me, I'm up a creek.
I think I'll play hide and seek.
The whole world's on our back.

I know that you are feeling blue.
Your antidepressant is just about due.
But I wish it was for me instead of you.
The whole world's on our back.

CHAPTER 5

A Client's Perspective

Counselors encourage client growth and development in ways that foster the interest and welfare of clients and promote formation of healthy relationships. Counselors actively attempt to understand the diverse cultural backgrounds of the clients they serve. Counselors also explore their own cultural identities and how these affect their values and beliefs about the counseling process.

— *ACA Code of Ethics*, A. Introduction

Previous chapters considered the perspectives of the attorney, the auditor, and the coworker. However, the *ACA Code* clearly states, "The primary responsibility of counselors is to respect the dignity and to promote the welfare of clients" (A.1.a.). This chapter, therefore, focuses on the perspective of the central and most vulnerable figure in the counseling process, the client. After all, it is his or her life that the counselor is writing about. And the most substantive and sensitive elements in that life may be, necessarily, included in the official record: background, family, relationships, education and work histories, medical history, and problems with social interaction or the law. The way that documentation is written directly affects treatment, but if read by the client, it may also affect the client's self-esteem and possibly become his or her basis for legal recourse against a professional.

The *Code* emphasizes a wide range of client privileges in the professional relationship:

- The client can choose whether to enter into or remain in a counseling relationship.
- The client is guaranteed adequate information about the counselor and the entire counseling process.
- The client is guaranteed both a written and verbal review of the counselor's and the client's rights and responsibilities. Informed consent is essential in the counseling process, and discussions of informed consent must be documented in accordance with the *Code*.

The first time a client is seen, it is not uncommon to say something like, "Mr. Johnson, I know this is a difficult time for you, but you are going to have to learn to trust and deal with feelings that you have been avoiding." As counseling progresses, the clients do trust. In fact, they may tell you things they have never told another human being. However, dissatisfied clients and former clients may see an attorney who convinces them to sue you or file allegations of unethical conduct. Their lawyer has a judge issue some orders, and the next thing you know, they get not all but a significant portion of what they consider to be their records as well as information from your personnel files.

If you wrote, "Mr. Johnson is evasive, impulsive, and appears to be manipulative and demanding," or described him as unmotivated, unresponsive, and showing poor judgment, did you discuss these issues with him? Did you let him know what was being placed in the record? Did you define the terms? Are they an accurate representation of his culture? Perhaps what you consider unmotivated and unresponsive is characteristic for his ethnicity.

If a client says he or she had three brief hospitalizations in 12 years, write that. It is inaccurate and unfair to enter a sentence such as, "Client has a history of hospitalizations." This gives the distinct impression of a more serious series of hospitalizations and also indicates more serious long-term problems. To be precise, list the specific number and length of each hospitalization and the reasons.

DOUBLE STANDARDS

No one likes being told what to do, and a counselor's entry can, perhaps, indicate a double standard as well as insensitivity to another's culture. For example, when a client speaks his or her mind, the record may describe the individual as aggressive or noncompliant. But when you or I express our feelings, we're being honest and open. When clients want to be left alone, they have been described as isolating themselves, but when you or I don't want to be around others, we take a "mental health day" to relax. When we talk to a stranger, we are considered friendly, but counseling records may indicate this behavior in the client is inappropriate. Most of us do not like being told what to do, but clients are often described as disruptive and resistive. Perhaps they are being assertive.

It is not uncommon for a counselor to ask a client if she or he ever experienced hallucinations. When the client's answer is "No," do not write, "Mr. Johnson denies hallucinations." *Deny* is an interesting word, and it has several meanings. One definition is that the individual refuses to accept, admit, or acknowledge truth and reality. The counselor does not have a right to imply the existence of hallucinations, unless other entries in the record can confirm the problem. Sometimes *deny* is the appropriate word to use in describing a client, but be careful where and how you use this term.

Counselors often write about the client's family members. I recall reading about a wife who was supposed to take her husband (the client) to a vocational rehabilitation office for psychological testing, but she didn't get him there. The entry said, "Mrs. Johnson, like her husband, refuses to follow through." In reality, however, she did not refuse, because to *refuse* means to willingly withhold compliance. On the day of that scheduled appointment, the client's favorite niece died in an automobile accident, so according to cultural precedent, he and his wife spent the day with the child's mother trying to console her.

CULTURAL DIVERSITY

In our multicultured society it is important for counselors to be more aware than ever of the variety of ethnicities within which we live and work. This portion of the monograph, therefore, will address cultural diversity. Once again, as we turn to the *Code* for direction, we are reminded that, "Counselors recognize that support networks hold various meanings in the lives of clients and consider enlisting the support, understanding, and involvement of others (e.g., religious/

spiritual/community leaders, family members, friends) as positive resources, when appropriate, with client consent" (A.1.d.).

Cultural competence and social diversity means understanding the function of culture in human behavior and recognizing the strengths in all cultures. The *Code* stipulates that you must have a basic knowledge of the clients' cultures and be able to provide services that are sensitive to their cultural groups. In other words, you must be aware of your biases and prejudices. It is essential to know the limitations of what you can or cannot do. Likewise it is essential to know when you need to refer clients to another counselor.

A professional associate shared the following scenario with me: You are the assigned counselor for an American-born, female Vietnamese teenager. Her parents were born and reared in Vietnam, speak limited English, and complain that their daughter is disobeying rules, having problems in school, hanging around with bad kids, and not helping care for her grandmother, who also resides in the home. Some of the questions an ethical professional would consider are these:

- What is the extent of your knowledge of Vietnamese culture? What impact will such knowledge (or lack of it) have on the quality of your service? If you know little, where and how can you learn more?
- Would it make a difference if you were Vietnamese? If yes, would it make a difference if you were born and reared in Vietnam or America?
- If you're not Vietnamese, what feelings (if any) of your own do you need to manage?
- What is the client's preferred language? Are linguistic abilities addressed as a part of treatment and documented? For example, if your organization treats people of a certain ethnic group, are forms available in the appropriate language?
- Is the client dependent upon a family member or friend to translate?
- What about immigration status? Do you understand the reasons a client had for leaving his or her country of origin?
- Is there a trust issue regarding the client's fear that information might be shared with a government agency and lead to deportation?

- Does the client affiliate primarily with people of his or her culture? Why? Why not?
- Have I correctly identified the client's ethnic background rather than made assumptions? How will I address issues of ethnic differences?

It is important to know something about the culture being dealt with and understand that within some cultures, there may be different values relating to authority and respect. The counselor's role is not to side with one family member or another, but rather to facilitate communication and reduce or eliminate family discord.

The *Code* does not require that you know everything about every culture, race, religion, and ethnic group, but rather that you demonstrate competence by accepting the fact that differences will always exist and having the ability to discuss differences.

Cultural competence also relates to differences in how people communicate. The record should contain documentation to verify a counselor's discussion related to pertinent cultural issues. The *Code* emphasizes the importance of communication: "Counselors use clear and understandable language when discussing issues related to informed consent. When clients have difficulty understanding the language used by counselors, they provide necessary services (e.g., arrange for a qualified interpreter or translator) to ensure comprehension by clients. In collaboration with clients, counselors consider cultural implications of informed consent procedures and, where possible, counselors adjust their practices accordingly" (A.2.c.).

Obviously, this is a complex issue. Remember, too, unethical conduct can surface in the form of unmanaged countertransference (i.e., having prejudices and allowing those prejudices to enter into the treatment setting or perpetuating negative beliefs of specific groups with comments like, "Those people are all alike").

Another professional colleague told me he is not sure how to "demonstrate cultural competence," but he shared a situation from which we can all learn. His work with a Hispanic group gave him a basic knowledge of this culture, but he admitted that in some respects, he may be "short-changing" the clients because of limited knowledge. His goal is to do the best he can to provide a service that would not otherwise be available in the community. He assured me that if a Hispanic group became available with a qualified professional, he would make an immediate referral. He's had clients from Iran, Iraq, and Bosnia and admits he cannot possibly know everything about their cultures, so he asks questions about their values and refrains from making moral judgments about issues such as sexual preference, abortion, death, dress codes, and foods. He also recalled a client from Appalachia who showed no emotion after the death of a close friend. His research into Appalachian culture taught him that the client's "flat affect" was a cultural pattern rather than a symptom of a mental illness. That sort of approach is in compliance with the spirit of any code of ethics.

My obligation in this monograph is to remind you of your responsibility to make an effort to understand a client's culture. But let's be realistic; no one person can be an expert for every culture. I recall receiving a child abuse report from an English-speaking neighbor, but no one in the "offending" family could speak English. After legal consultation, the agency contracted with an interpreter who was familiar with the language and the culture. We made a home visit to make an assessment and confirmed that there was no child abuse.

In summary, our responsibility is to accept people, not judge them. To ensure compliance with the *Code*, you may need to obtain education about the nature of social diversity with respect to race, ethnicity, sex, marriage, religion, and physical disability. Don't forget to document all such activity in your personnel chart. List the session date, title, length, and a brief description of the course as well as the name and credentials of the trainer.

The ethical professional can trust his or her own good sense of decency and respect for others. When such a professional demonstrates the qualities discussed in this chapter, those qualities will come through to any client.

Online Counseling
and Electronic Records

When providing technology-assisted distance counseling services, counselors determine that clients are intellectually, emotionally, and physically capable of using the application and that the application is appropriate for the needs of clients.
—ACA Code of Ethics, A.12.b.

Counselors take precautions to ensure the confidentiality of information transmitted through the use of computers, electronic mail, facsimile machines, telephones, voicemail, answering machines, and other electronic or computer technology.
—ACA Code of Ethics, B.3.e.

Since publication of the previous edition of this monograph in 2001, electronic technology has exploded and has made the requirements for online counseling and electronic records even more challenging for every helping profession. In addition, since the 1996 passage of the Health Insurance Portability and Accountability Act (HIPAA), there has been an ongoing controversy about the storage and transmission of electronic data as well as various interpretations of pertinent law.

Counselors, therefore, are rightly concerned about these complex sets of regulations. Both areas are crucial to the client–counselor relationship: with online counseling you speak directly to the client via the Internet, while with electronic records you document your interventions and judgments.

This monograph cannot resolve the myriad of confidentiality concerns or provide you with a comprehensive understanding of the wide range of technical and legal issues involved in the professional's use of electronic communications. Our overall topic is substantive documentation and ethical conduct. To obtain a full understanding of technical and legal guidelines, you are referred to the complete HIPAA text (see References, Suggested Readings, and Web Sites); your code of ethics; recognized, knowledgeable professionals; and related publications. Nevertheless, this chapter attempts to focus on some basic guidelines, using some of these sources as well as related personal experiences and resources.

ONLINE COUNSELING SERVICES AND SAFEGUARDS

An increasing number of professionals are using the Internet to provide counseling services, for general correspondence with clients, and for correspondence with other professionals about specific clients. A professional associate in vocational counseling says, "I share job leads and things like this with a client because it is fast and efficient, but beyond that I do not provide counseling by e-mail because too much can be lost in the translation. Without the voice to give emphasis and empathy, some remarks can come across as cold." He also says some of his coworkers believe it is acceptable to share and communicate much more information, but he's not sure of the pros and cons of Internet use. Candidly, neither am I. Regardless of the extent of your usage, caution and consultation are necessary before you use electronic media or online counseling.

If you are using or considering using the Internet to provide online counseling, the *ACA Code* has specific standards:

- Confirm that your liability insurance provides coverage for online counseling.
- Confirm that the provision of such service is not prohibited by state or local statutes, your profession's code, or state licensing boards.
- Confirm that the use of technology does not violate the laws of any local, state, national, or international entity, and observe all relevant statutes.

- Evaluate and confirm the appropriateness of online counseling services, ensuring that clients are intellectually, emotionally, and physically capable of using the technology.
- Provide clients with reasonable access to computer applications, a schedule of times when services are available (including response times), and an alternate means of contacting you in the event of an emergency.
- Seek assistance from legal and technical experts, particularly when the use of electronic technology crosses state or national boundaries.

The *Code* calls attention to the difference between secure and nonsecure sites. To ensure confidentiality, one-on-one (or group) counseling should be provided only through Web sites or e-mails with encryption. When encryption is not possible, advise clients of this fact and limit electronic transmissions to general communications (i.e., information that is not client-specific).

In addition to encryption software, file servers with firewalls can help protect client information. Other protective measures include saving online (or e-mail) communications to your hard drive or file server, creating regularly scheduled backup copies on a diskette or CD, or printing paper copies of all electronic communications.

Informed Consent and Confidentiality

Whether you provide services face to face or through electronic media, the requirements for informed consent remain of paramount importance. Professionals who use online counseling will find that, once again, the *Code* is an excellent source for guidance. The standards require that you ensure clients are provided with information about technology limitations and possible abuses. Ethical counselors will address issues related to the difficulty of maintaining the confidentiality of electronically transmitted communications and inform clients that unauthorized persons, including clients' family members, may have access to sensitive information.

Remember, even placing a client's name in an e-mail provides an opportunity for breach of confidentiality because all information can be "forwarded" to someone who has no right or need to know. And, if the wrong address is used, information will be sent to someone who does not have the right or need to know. Your options include using initials only or first name and last initial.

Before obtaining the client's written informed consent, discuss the possibility of technology failure and alternative methods of service delivery. Equally important is the need to inform clients when online counseling is not covered by insurance.

Most importantly, it is your responsibility to ensure that clients are intellectually, emotionally, and physically capable of using online counseling services. That means your intake procedure must be capable of determining whether online counseling is appropriate for the needs of the client.

Assuming you have determined that online counseling is appropriate, the client should be required to provide written informed consent, stating that he or she acknowledges the limitations inherent in ensuring the confidentiality of online information. The client must also agree to waive the privilege of confidentiality with respect to information that may be accessed by any third party without authorization and despite your efforts to provide a secure system. If the client is unable or unwilling to consent to such an agreement, refer him or her to more traditional methods of counseling. Failing to do so will certainly increase your risk exposure for a lawsuit or allegations of unethical conduct.

Another critically important component is identity verification that ensures you receive information from and send information to only the acknowledged client. To find out how your software confirms identity verification, discuss this issue with an IT (information technology) specialist or a knowledgeable person in your organization.

A final crucial issue of legal and ethical importance relates to the client's age. A counselor must verify that the person is above the age of minority, competent to enter into a therapeutic relationship, and able to give informed consent. In my opinion, that means at least one face-to-face session before online counseling begins. In the event clients are minor children, incompetent, or incapable of giving informed consent, obtain written consent from the legal guardian or other authorized legal representative before online counseling begins.

Online counseling is fraught with problems, and for this reason I urge comprehensive planning, utmost caution, and never-ending vigilance to ensure accuracy and confidentiality.

Counselor Web Sites

Counselors who have a Web site or who are considering the use of one must also keep the following points in mind:

- Check links regularly to ensure accuracy. Appropriate links include, but are not limited to, state licensure and professional certification boards.
- Offer accessibility to persons with disabilities and provide translation capabilities for clients who have a different first language.
- Provide notices to inform clients of the security and encryption status of the site, the need for special software, and the availability of software from the counselor, if necessary.
- Provide readily visible notices advising clients of the identities of all other professionals who will have access to information and the manner by which clients may direct information to a particular professional counselor for those in a group practice. Professional counselors inform clients if any or all of the sessions are supervised and if and how the session transcripts are preserved. Background information on all professionals with access to the online communications must also be provided (i.e., education, licensing, and certification).

ELECTRONIC RECORD-KEEPING GUIDELINES

Whether you use paper or an electronic medium, the following points will always remain valid:

- Service providers need timely, accurate, and comprehensive information. Lack of information can impede quality of care because the decision-making process is placed at risk.
- An organization must comply with its own written policy related to record keeping and confidentiality. In the event of litigation or allegations of unethical conduct, "failure to comply" can be used against the service provider.
- One way to avoid misuse of information is to have trained employees who are committed to protecting the privacy of each client.

Whether you write on a piece of paper or make an entry into an electronic record, it is useful to make eight assumptions:

1. The counseling record will be subpoenaed and the court must understand what went on. I may or may not be with the agency when it happens.
2. Someone else will have to read and understand what I write because I may be sick or on vacation, or there may be an emergency when I am not available.
3. Legislation that opens a record to the client exists now or will be passed. In fact, the *Code* already provides the client with reasonable access to records.
4. I cannot be as accurate if I wait days or weeks to write a note, so I'll do it today.
5. This note will be the best possible reflection of my professional abilities.
6. No contact is considered a professional service until my entry is in the record.
7. This entry will be selected by the Division of Audits to verify a legally reimbursable service as defined by the funding source.
8. My service documentation and personnel file will be requested by the Board of Inquiry in the event of allegations of unethical conduct. The *Code* also requires that counselors cooperate with investigations.

Accessibility and Confidentiality

One area in which there is a vast difference between paper records stored in the conventional way and electronic records is accessibility. Electronically stored information is potentially accessible by countless numbers of people. The most comprehensive security system can fail when unethical or disgruntled employees and external hackers obtain information. The patchwork of state and federal laws does not provide 100% protection to anyone. Unfortunately, you can be reasonably sure that someone who has no right to information can obtain it and misuse it. Nevertheless, computerized information and the Internet are here to stay, even in such an information-sensitive area as counseling.

The following news story is an example of what can happen when an unethical professional abuses confidential electronic information: An employee of a nationally known charitable organization stole the identities of 40 clients and used the information to get more than $250,000 in cash and merchandise. The employee simply used electronic records to obtain names, addresses, dates of birth, social security numbers, telephone numbers, and places of employment to obtain credit, cash counterfeit checks, and get fraudulent bank loans.

That employee did much more by creating doubts in the minds of future donors and by damaging public trust about how confidential information is handled. The full extent of damage can never be determined. Any professional who engages in this kind of behavior and makes the headlines damages the credibility of all helping professionals, because the unethical actions of one person will always have an extended negative impact.

The potential for other breaches of confidentiality for personal gain is present in a recent national proposal for the establishment of an electronic network designed to store the medical information of over 100,000 patients. The goal, of course, is to reduce medication errors and provide instant, accurate information in emergencies. However, the admirable ambitions of such a program can be destroyed by the actions of one unethical individual. Indeed, electronic records provide a fertile environment for abuse.

Confidentiality issues are legitimate concerns because digital technologies have compromised the privacy of each individual who receives a service. As organizations and private practitioners increase their dependence on paperless records, the risk for improper access and disclosure increases. There is also the danger that a virus can intentionally or inadvertently alter or delete electronic data.

There must be a security component that ensures the protection of confidential information. Not everyone has a need or right to know what is contained in a client's file, so care must be taken to establish, document, and adhere to a clear-cut access procedure. Levels of priority to access client information must be established, and clearance to access data must be authorized in accordance with job title / responsibilities. A priority level would also determine who could enter new data, edit existing data, delete data, or simply view it. When one staff person can edit or delete the information entered by another individual, the integrity of the data is compromised and staff relations can become strained because one person believes information is clinically significant while another does not. You may even decide to maintain a paper record or log that verifies any modification of the information after it was originally entered in the electronic record. Perhaps a supervisor should be required to sign a form authorizing any change(s).

Your system should have not only password protection but also the capability of verifying who is logged on, who was logged on, who was denied access, dates and time of user activity, what data were printed by each user, and what work stations were involved. Each user should be provided with one code to log on to an information system and another code or password to actually access confidential client data.

Integrity of Data

The record will contain information about an individual and therefore should be an accurate reflection of the client, not a "canned" or prepackaged script that is so vague that entries could have been written about anyone who ever sought health care or human services. A system must permit staff to edit suggested sentences in a prepackaged plan, review, assessment, staff note, or any other clinical entry. Many organizations have developed formats that meet specific needs and reflect a client's differences, goals, and problem areas. The system you choose should permit you to use and perhaps strengthen existing forms. Systems that limit text entries not only deny the counselor an opportunity to enter more than one or two lines of information but also generate staff frustration since there is no room to enter data that are considered clinically significant.

If you are going to rely on electronic records, it will be imperative to provide training and supervision at all levels of staffing. When individuals with poor typing skills are responsible for data entry, reliability and usefulness will be adversely affected, thereby increasing your risk exposure.

Information from a variety of fields or screens must be consistent to ensure confidence. Contradictory information can indicate staff incompetence or lack of data integrity. When section A lists one diagnosis and section B lists a different diagnosis, the quality of care is compromised. If one field says the client is single but another field says the client is married, a reader or user will become confused. When screen F indicates the client is living with relatives while screen G indicates the client is living alone in an apartment, confusion results. What is a reader to believe and act on?

All computer systems crash now and then, so on a regularly scheduled basis, use disks or CDs to back up counseling data. To ensure accuracy, consider the use of a program that automatically includes the date of data entry as well as the authorized signature of the service provider.

In an age of ever-increasing information technology, counselors must exercise caution when selecting data for inclusion in the record. As other sections of this monograph point out, too much information equates to breach of confidentiality. I used to joke about getting a hernia from trying to lift a three-volume, 30-pound chart. Although a disk or CD will not weigh 30 pounds, it is possible to enter so much information that it becomes incomprehensible.

Use of electronic record-keeping systems may not always enable the counselor to save time or spend more time providing services. But these systems can eliminate errors caused by such things as illegible handwriting. As I was preparing the second edition of this monograph in 2001, a state court was considering a case involving a doctor's and a pharmacist's liability. The pharmacist was unable to read the doctor's handwriting and provided medication that resulted in the patient's death. A jury found the doctor, the pharmacist, and the pharmacy guilty of medical negligence and awarded $450,000 actual damages ("Teresa Vasquez," 1999).

Poor handwriting is unconscionable and potentially harmful in the counseling profession. Some clinical entries appear to be a misplaced Rorschach. Illegible entries may endanger the lives of clients and others in the community. There are no known national statistics to confirm that patients are being harmed, but more than 40 years of experience and continuous news coverage indicate the problem is all too common. As I was writing this third edition, one pharmacy group was even requiring that a physician print all prescription information in addition to providing a signature.

This monograph does not and cannot establish a fail-safe system of electronic record keeping or provide an approved list of the kinds of information that may be shared with other professionals electronically without risk. The final decision is yours, and whatever you decide, you must also assume full responsibility for the outcome. However, it is imperative that information be transferred to authorized third-party recipients only when two conditions are met: (1) both the professional with the information and the authorized recipient have secure transfer and acceptance communication capabilities and (2) the client's informed written consent has been obtained to acknowledge the limits of Internet confidentiality.

For counseling professionals to take advantage of the best and most current technology, we must obtain comprehensive and ongoing training in appropriate and discipline-specific software. Electronic records responsibly used and monitored will best serve both the counselor and the client of the future.

Although electronic systems were designed to eliminate or reduce paperwork, it is likely that we will rely on paper, to some extent, for years to come. Since so much time is spent on paperwork, even if it is electronic paper, I conclude here with one of my humorous workshop songs that recognizes the difficult job of a counselor.

Tons of Paperwork

(Chorus) You write 16 tons and what do you get?
Another day older and stiff in the neck!
Saint Peter don't you call me to the bright shore.
I still have to do a whole lot more.

I got to the office in the nick of time.
Three emergencies standing in line.
Sally and Jim had called in sick and
when the day ended I was ready for a trip
(to the nearest mental hospital).

Eighty-nine cases that need a plan.
At the end of a day, I can hardly stand.
But I'll tell you one thing that's tried and true.
I feel real good about the job I do.

If you see me coming you'd better step aside.
I'm trained and ready, filled with pride.
I'll do my job day after day, and believe it or not,
in spite of the pay.

CHAPTER 7

Sexual Relationships and Dual Relationships

Sexual or romantic counselor–client interactions or relationships with current clients, their romantic partners, or their family members are prohibited.

—*ACA Code of Ethics,* A.5.a.

Sexual or romantic counselor–research participant interactions or relationships with current research participants are prohibited.

—*ACA Code of Ethics,* G.3.b.

The counselor–client relationship is a profoundly personal one, obviously. In such a relationship, the client may have shared confidences never before shared with anyone. It is easy to understand, therefore, how this relationship could evolve into a friendship, or in some cases, even a romantic or sexual relationship. But as the above quotations from the *ACA Code* indicate, sexual or romantic relationships are strictly prohibited. This chapter explores the complexities of the principles related to sexual and dual relationships.

SEXUAL RELATIONSHIPS AND ETHICAL CONDUCT

As I was working on this edition of the monograph, the daily newspaper was a constant reminder of those complexities. Consider the following news stories and ask yourself how important the documentation in the counseling record and the personnel file will be in the event of allegations of unethical behavior or a malpractice lawsuit:

- A circuit court jury awarded $2 million to a former hospital patient who accused a certified nursing assistant of raping her 3 years earlier. The employee said the sex was consensual, but attorneys contended that the employee had a criminal history and never should have been hired and that the hospital did not provide a safe place for patients. The employee's public records included information about his fight with a family member, a conviction for unemployment fraud, and charges involving another incidence of domestic violence. Attorneys for the plaintiff said the hospital "violated its own policies and procedures," and they won.
- A sexual abuse suit against an adolescent residential care program alleged staff indifference to sexual contact between clients. The mother who brought the suit said she thought the program was a safe place for her son to get help but that the experience hurt him.
- A counselor was charged with 15 counts of illegal and unethical behavior including using unacceptable procedures, touching female clients in a way that caused "emotional discomfort and confusion," and making inappropriate remarks about his own sexuality. The counselor explained a technique that encouraged women to view him as their father, sitting women on his lap, holding hands, and kissing their cheeks. One woman said, "I trusted him. And just like other key people in my life, he broke the trust." Another woman said, "I went to him for help, and I got hurt worse than I've ever been hurt in my life."

Although most codes of ethics have sections that may leave room for interpretation, sections referring to sexual relationships never leave room for doubt. The bottom line is this:

- Do not, under any circumstances, engage in sexual activities or sexual contact with current clients, whether such contact is consensual or forced.
- Do not engage in sexual activities or sexual contact with clients' relatives or other individuals with whom clients maintain a personal relationship.

- Do not provide services to any individual with whom you have had a prior sexual relationship.

These directives refer to current clients, but the *Code* also specifically refers to relationships with former clients. The *Code* mandates a period of 5 years following the last professional contact before a romantic relationship can be considered. This refers not only to former clients but also to their romantic partners or family members. Counselors are cautioned to "demonstrate forethought and document (in written form) whether the interactions or relationship can be viewed as exploitive in some way and/or whether there is still potential to harm the former client" (A.5.b.). If the counselor decides potential harm exists, such a relationship must be avoided.

Although this standard opens the door to a sexual relationship, extreme caution and thoughtful consideration are suggested before entering into such a relationship. Assuming the role of devil's advocate, I offer the following recommendations for your consideration: Do not engage in sexual activities or sexual contact with former clients; if you engage in a sexual relationship because you believe an exception is warranted, it is you, not the client, who must be able to demonstrate that he or she was not exploited, forced, or unduly influenced, intentionally or unintentionally. Although it might be argued that the *Code* allows you to use professional judgment about whether to initiate a sexual relationship, in my opinion, even after 5 years, it is a high-risk venture. Some professionals may also make a case that relationships within certain settings should be exempt from such scrutiny because those relationships are not therapeutic. Regardless of your profession, before deciding and acting, ask yourself this question, "What is the worst possible thing that can happen if the relationship turns sour?" One important fact to remember is that in instances of unethical allegations, state licensing and disciplinary boards, not you, will interpret the *Code* and determine the final outcome.

The *ACA Code* extends beyond counselors' sexual relationships with clients, saying supervisors must not engage in sexual activities or sexual contact with supervisees, students, trainees, or other colleagues over whom they exercise professional authority.

Sexual Harassment

Sexual harassment is another matter on which the *Code* is clear. Because harassment cases have proliferated over the past years, it will be wise for every professional to review the specific recommendations about sexual harassment in his or her code.

The *ACA Code* defines sexual harassment as "sexual solicitation, physical advances, or verbal or nonverbal conduct that is sexual in nature, that occurs in connection with professional activities or roles, and that either (1) is unwelcome, is offensive, or creates a hostile workplace or learning environment, and counselors know or are told this; or (2) is sufficiently severe or intense to be perceived as harassment to a reasonable person in the context in which the behavior occurred" (C.6.a.). Given this definition, counselors must not engage in or condone sexual harassment.

The *Code* explicitly refers to interactions with supervisees and cautions against accepting close relatives, romantic partners, or friends as supervisees. Additionally, ethical counselors do not sexually harass colleagues. In fact, they never harass anyone, not only because it is wrong, but also because it is a violation of Title 7 of the Civil Rights Act of 1964. Harassment includes sexual advances, sexual solicitation, requests for sexual favors, and verbal or physical conduct of a sexual nature. Physical contact might also be construed as sexual harassment.

Forty-five years ago, when I entered the social services profession, there was no code of ethics. But today's counselors have a code, and it says that we do not engage in physical contact such as cradling or caressing clients when there is a possibility of psychological harm to the client as a result of the contact. Professionals who use physical contact are responsible for setting clear and culturally sensitive boundaries that govern the contact.

Years ago touch was not the issue it is today. For example, we know a hug can be a comforting human experience, and it is a common, accepted behavior in most situations involving family or friends. But physical contact is a different matter within a professional, helping relationship. It is also complicated by the fact that a client may interpret the contact in a way that was not intended. The lack of touch, however, can also be problematic. One powerful song I know deals with school children accustomed to receiving a hug for good grades or behavior. Suddenly, a memo is sent to all teachers forbidding hugs. The children become confused and assume they have been bad and that is why they are no longer hugged. Another compelling song is about a mental health professional working in a hospital where electroshock therapy is used but the staff is prohibited from hugging patients because it is viewed as sexual sublimation. One verse says, "You can strap 'em and zap 'em with electroshock, but you'd better not give them a hug."

DUAL RELATIONSHIPS IN THE COUNSELING PROCESS

It can be very easy to become friends with a client, but the *Code* warns against dual relationships. Let's assume your client enjoys going to a basketball game and you have an extra ticket. When you invite a client to join you, a dual relationship exists. Should you invite a client to dinner or should the client invite you to dinner, a dual relationship exists.

It can be an effortless process for anyone to rationalize or justify a dual relationship, but the simple fact is this: when you are in a friendship relationship as well as a clinical relationship, you are also in a dual relationship. Professionals do not engage in dual or multiple relationships with clients or former clients when there is a risk of exploitation or potential harm to the client. The problem, of course, is determining the risk of exploitation. In instances in which dual or multiple relationships are unavoidable, the primary obligation is to protect the client. You are responsible for setting clear and culturally sensitive boundaries.

Unavoidable Dual Relationships

Unavoidable dual relationships exist more often in rural areas with a small population because you are more likely to be involved with someone not only as a client but also as a member of the community in which both you and the client live. However, whether you live in a small town or the big city, you have the ethical responsibility of establishing boundaries early on. You might say something like, "If we meet in a public setting, we will not talk about your situation." Better yet, why not ask what the client prefers you do or not do. Years ago, I should have taken my own advice. One night, I literally bumped into a client at a college basketball game. Seeing him there was a sign of progress because he had few friends and usually isolated himself in a small apartment. I was so pleased to see him, I spoke to him and said I hoped he enjoyed the game. The next morning he came to my office. He was angry and said I had no right to recognize him in a public place. It embarrassed him because people knew I was a social worker and he did not want anyone to know that he knew someone at the mental health clinic. I was wrong, and he had a right to be angry.

In another situation it is possible that you might provide service to two or more people who have a relationship with each other, for example, couples and family members. Here are some suggestions to consider:

- Clarify with all parties which individuals will be considered clients.
- Clarify the nature of your professional obligations to the various individuals who are receiving services, particularly if you anticipate a conflict of interest among the individuals receiving services or you anticipate having to perform in potentially conflicting roles.

An associate I know always relinquishes any future ability to render custody-related opinions when he becomes the assigned professional for one of the disputing parties. He informs attorneys, clients, and the court that he cannot be objective after offering services to one or several members of the family. However, with a client's permission, he does agree to provide pertinent factual information such as service dates.

Providing services to members of the same family or to a client's significant other can also be problematic. Another associate said she phoned a client (a young woman) but one of her other clients (an older woman) answered the phone. Until that moment the professional had no idea the two women were mother and daughter because of different last names. Interestingly, neither the mother nor the daughter knew they were seeing the same counselor. The call was innocent, but as you can imagine, in some cases such an encounter could result in serious relationship problems. To maintain confidentiality and ensure positive relationships, you might consider cross-referencing phone numbers, addresses, and married names, etc.

Speaking of confidentiality, it may be best not to leave detailed information on phone message machines unless the client has authorized you to do so. Even leaving your name, the agency name, and phone number will alert anyone listening about a relationship with a counseling agency. Still another associate recalled an occasion when a client left two phone contact numbers. When the professional called one and was told the client no longer lived there, she asked if the other number she had was correct. As it turned out, the client was trying to separate from a boyfriend and had not given him the other phone number. The client was upset that the professional inadvertently disclosed an unlisted number. The professional apologized, but the client had not shared all the circumstances with the professional.

Potentially Beneficial Dual Relationships

Multiple relationships (other than romantic or sexual), however, may be appropriate in some situations. Once again, the *ACA Code of Ethics*, our most important source document, cautions that even these relationships with clients, former clients, their romantic partners, or their family members "should be avoided, except when the interaction is potentially beneficial to the client" (A.5.c.). The problem now becomes determining what constitutes a potentially beneficial interaction. To be honest, the *Code* places the responsibility for answering this question squarely on the counselor's shoulders. Nonetheless, it does provide some helpful examples: attending a wedding or graduation, purchasing a product provided by a client or former client, visiting an ill client or family member in the hospital, or sharing a membership in a community organization.

If the counselor decides to enter into this kind of relationship, he or she must obtain client consent and document the rationale for the decision. In the counselor–client relationship, a counselor is assumed to be the healthy person, and the client is the vulnerable person. Therefore, the full burden for maintaining a healthy relationship must be the counselor's.

CHAPTER 8

Documenting High-Risk Cases

Counselors understand the ACA Code of Ethics *and other applicable ethics codes from other professional organizations or from certification and licensure bodies of which they are members. Lack of knowledge or misunderstanding of an ethical responsibility is not a defense against a charge of unethical conduct.*
— ACA Code of Ethics, *H.1.a.*

Risk is an ever-present reality in the counseling arena. As previous chapters have indicated, immunity from legal liability has almost disappeared. The possibility of legal or fiscal losses resulting from inadequate documentation offers a compelling reason to ensure that records are precise and current. Counselors tend to be optimistic and do not anticipate being involved in costly, possibly ugly, legal disputes. But as the bumper sticker says, "Stuff happens!" Records are vital to reconstruct the course of treatment, particularly in high-risk cases. Among such cases are those involving violence, threats of violence, homicide, suicide, potential suicide, physical and sexual abuse, and criminal behavior. Your best defense when dealing with such cases is to be prepared.

Some issues are not resolvable to everyone's satisfaction, and documentation is one such issue. You will not be able to create a chart that will satisfy every human being. Nevertheless, I hope this chapter provides useful ideas for you to build on when documenting high-risk cases.

QUALIFIERS, VIOLENCE, AND THREATS OF VIOLENCE

If you write, "This client may be dangerous," you must do three things: (a) explain how you reached the conclusion, (b) act, and (c) document the action. Action options include but are not limited to (a) notifying a potential target and/or the appropriate law enforcement agency, (b) consulting with a psychiatrist, (c) completing a case review, and (d) considering an involuntary hospitalization. Inaction must be explained. For example, if you choose not to warn an intended target, document the reason(s). Someone can always question your action or inaction, but at least you have established a defense.

HOMICIDAL AND SUICIDAL CLIENTS

When you believe someone may be homicidal or suicidal, put it in the record, but always explain how you reached the conclusion. This is easily done by using the client's own words or describing the behaviors.

When a client threatens to injure or kill someone, you may have a duty to warn the potential target. A counselor's obligation to maintain confidentiality will not apply when disclosure is necessary to prevent harm to the client or specifically named individual(s) or when state and federal laws require disclosure without client consent, such as in child abuse and elder abuse cases. In such instances, you should seek consultation with your coworkers, supervisor, and a lawyer and document those consultations in your record. Remarks about homicide and suicide must always be taken seriously and must always be documented.

The client may say he or she has no intention to harm self or others, but if your professional intuition or the content of the chart gives you cause for concern, this may be just the appropriate place to use a word like *appears* or *possibly* because no one can be sure of everything. Ask the client how he or she feels and use their words.

You cannot eliminate the use of all qualifiers, but eliminate them as often as possible. When records are filled with a preponderance of qualifiers, you could be judged incompetent or lose funding already received. There is no rule that says it is within acceptable limits to use *appears* three times a month, *seems* twice a month, and *possibly* one time a month. But these words create doubt, so use them sparingly.

I recall reading an assessment that contained 20 qualifiers. In one workshop example, there is a staff note with five qualifiers. It says, among other things, that the client seems satisfied, seems she wrote a letter, seems relaxed, seems to smile easily, and is possibly suicidal.

Let's discuss each one of those qualifications. When satisfaction and relaxation have clinical significance, do not qualify them. Say to the client, "You seem more satisfied than when you came in 6 months ago. How are you feeling?" If the person says, "I had not thought of it, but yes, I do feel more satisfied," then write it. Not only do you document progress, but you also eliminate the doubt. Good writing is said to be 80 to 90% listening. Write it just as you hear it. But if you put quotation marks on a page, the words must be exact, not approximations. How can you be sure it is exact? Keep it short, one phrase, and at the most, one sentence. I have read records containing paragraph after paragraph in quotes. That is not reasonable unless you can verify the session was recorded and this note is the official transcription.

Seems she wrote a letter? Seems to smile easily? If a letter and a smile have clinical significance, they should not be qualified. When there is no clinical relevance, who cares? Auditors, lawyers, and support staff who maintain records have told me when they read an assessment, plan, and subsequent notes, they cannot tell they are reading about the same person. Too often, notes ramble about a series of events or problems that have no relationship to previous entries. The next time you prepare to write an entry, ask yourself, "Does this sentence have anything to do with the problems or goals listed in the most recent plan or the initial assessment?" If your answer is yes, write it. If your answer is no, you may be able to leave it out.

There is a caution, however, because clients' lives can and do change from one contact to the next. I recall working with a person who was preparing to return to the job market after a series of psychiatric hospitalizations. Therefore, all problems and goals were related to specific vocational issues. One day, however, he came to my office upset and crying. He said, "I do not want to live any longer. Every time I make an investment of myself in someone, they leave me or they die! I can't take the pain and rejection anymore! I'd be better off dead." Based on what I said about relating the note to the plan, do you think I would have said, "You have not been on time once this week. You are not taking the medication as it was prescribed and your breaks have been too long." No. And I do not believe you would either. After a series of questions, I learned his dog had died the previous night. I also discovered the dog had died on the same night his mother had died the previous year. I helped him recognize that his emotional hurt was natural and due in part to the anniversary syndrome. I assisted with unfinished grief work. That was the service and that is what I wrote. What does that have to do with vocational skills? Nothing! So use your best judgment. If, however, my client becomes obsessed with loss and dying, I need a case review that lists the new problem and goal.

What about that phrase "possibly suicidal"? Does it fit a person who "seems satisfied, relaxed, and smiles easily"? The possibility of suicidal behavior is the single most important issue requiring a counselor's clarification. If you are not there tomorrow and I have to see this person, I need to know what the person was feeling and what you did. Ask! If the person says, "I am so depressed I'm killing myself tonight," we know. And we eliminate qualifiers like *possibly*.

But a client might say, "Don't worry about me. I know I overreact. I will not hurt myself or anyone else." If your professional intuition or other information in the chart causes concern and you are not sure, it is probably best to use words like *may be suicidal* or *possibly suicidal*. But do not forget that when you write the word *suicidal* or *homicidal*, you must also let a reader know how you reached this conclusion, and you must act.

Once you make an entry regarding the possibility of a high-risk behavior, you impose legal obligations on yourself and you must act, for example, by alerting a potential target or considering an involuntary commitment. Whatever action you take, document it. If the last note in your record indicates the person might harm self or other, and the client follows through, your defense is very limited because a professional should know better than to let a "possibly suicidal person" walk away. The legal case against a counselor in this instance is called *abandonment*.

Someone sent me a news article that read, "A federal aviation spokesperson said the crash could have been caused by the wings falling off the plane." I rest my case about the use of qualifiers.

PHYSICAL AND SEXUAL ABUSE

When you have reason to suspect abuse, neglect, or criminal behavior, discuss the case with a lawyer and contact the appropriate law enforcement agency if the law requires a report. Good documentation is critical and entries should be made on the same date as the event. Content should clearly confirm the action taken and the outcome (if any).

When physical, emotional, or sexual abuse is suspected, extreme caution must be taken. The best approach is to document the client's words and behaviors, rather than express an unfounded opinion or suspicion.

I recall attending a workshop in which an attorney read a letter from a young girl who said she had been raped by her mother's boyfriend. The note pleaded, "Please don't tell anyone. He says he will kill my mother and me. Get the police. I need help." Such documentation clearly provides a reader with the client's concern.

When an abused child is in therapy, the child's attorney and the child's therapist must work hand in hand for the child's interest. The counselor should attempt to have records sealed or reviewed only by the judge to determine if anything is relevant.

CRIMINAL BEHAVIOR

When a client admits committing a crime or reveals an intention to commit a crime, you will have ethical and legal decisions to make. Clients must be advised that confidentiality has its limits and that the law requires a counselor to report child abuse, elder abuse, and threats against another's life, for example (see *Tarasoff v. Board of Regents*, 1976).

Even though a client may be psychotic, destruction of property, harassment, and violence or threats of violence are criminal behaviors. You have an obligation to protect yourself, other staff, other clients, and the general public. Depending on the degree of seriousness of these actions or threats of action, calling the police for assistance may be appropriate and necessary. After an arrest or other court disposition, counseling may still be needed and offered. In such cases, documentation is of utmost importance. However, this monograph cannot assist you in making a determination about continuing to serve the client. A counselor makes this decision based only on his or her professional judgment and the specifics of the individual case.

PERMISSION FOR SERVICE FORM

Whether the case is high risk or not, one basic form is important: the permission for service or the consent for treatment. State licensure law often specifies the contents of this form. This document is the client's or the client's legal representative's authorization for you to provide service. The signature is of utmost importance, and several considerations must be involved. Is the client's level of functioning sufficient for him or her to know what is being signed? Will the chart verify it? Is the client legally competent to sign? If not, do you have a copy of the court order?

Extreme caution must be taken if the client is a minor. Do you have a legal guardian's signature or a copy of the court order? In some states a minor can sign for limited services: be sure you know what is acceptable in your state. Generally, a minor may consent to and receive limited treatment if the professional's best judgment is that the risk to life or health is of such a nature that treatment must be given without delay. Again, good documentation is essential.

Treatment should be given only after a client has signed a permission form. The length and complexity of the form, however, can be detriments. For example, an attorney may attempt to show that the client could not understand what was being signed because the forms were too confusing or the implications of those forms were not fully explained.

The permission for service form for an adult should contain at least the following elements:

- A statement such as, "Permission for service is hereby authorized for (counselor or organization) to render service/treatment to (name) whose relationship to me is (circle one) self, child, spouse, or other (be specific)"
- A statement such as, "I understand that (counselor or organization) may terminate services for noncompliance with the plan of care, failure to keep or cancel appointments, violent behavior, threats of violence, or involvement in criminal behavior" (Note: This item could be deleted from a consent form if the issue is explained in a rights and responsibilities statement that is given to every client.)

- The signature of the client or his or her legal representative if needed
- The signature of a witness if needed
- The date
- A statement such as, "A copy of this consent form was given to the client. (circle one) Yes No"

The permission for service form for a minor should contain essentially the same kind of information as just mentioned as well as specific reference to the legal status of the client, that is,

- married minor;
- married minor with child;
- emancipated minor (not financially supported by family and not under control of parents or any other guardian);
- minor in need of treatment for drug abuse or addiction or under the influence; or
- minor in need of immediate treatment and requiring parental or guardian consent (chart must contain specific data).

ADDITIONAL CONSIDERATIONS

1. In many states, the signature of a minor is not legally binding. Counselors must be aware of their state's statutes.
2. Do not ask clients to sign blank forms to be dated and used later.
3. Not all documentation is admissible in a court of law. So before you agree to take a counseling record to court, find out what is and what is not admissible in your state.
4. In an emergency or high-risk case, discuss your concerns with an attorney, document the consultation, and then act in accordance with the legal advice. Counselors may wish to keep their notes of consultation with the attorney in a separate chart. Then the consultation notes will be privileged until disclosed in accordance with prevailing law.
5. Stick to the facts and avoid statements that are impressionistic or defamatory. Avoid conclusionary words or undefined modifiers such as *homicidal, suicidal, delusional, dangerous, unfit, abusive,* and *violent*. Rather than use an adjective, translate the necessary information into a verb that clarifies an observable behavior.

6. Exercise caution when listing other individuals' names in a chart. For example, if someone is having an extramarital affair, do not record the lover's name. But it is appropriate to list names if you have consulted with an attorney, another counselor, or a school teacher.

7. Suicide and homicide contracts can be clinically useful because they verify the counselor's attempt to help the client understand the seriousness of a situation. However, in litigation, a contract does not always protect you.

8. *Delayed disclosure* is a complex and controversial issue. In a court of law, the plaintiff's attorney will challenge the validity of recovered memories and attempt to convince a jury that a counselor caused a client to generate false memories of events. Therefore, it is important to remember that documentation is not only a treatment tool but also a potential legal document that may be used against you. How good is your record keeping? What will it show about your approach, intervention, and technique?

   Don't forget that lives other than the client's can be affected. For example, a family member or someone in the community (such as a teacher or a neighbor) could initiate allegations of unethical conduct or a lawsuit against the counselor who is treating a client who claims to have been sexually abused by that person in childhood. This is dangerous territory, so the counselor must exercise caution. Clients could be experiencing flashbacks associated with posttraumatic stress syndrome. Document what you did and how you did it. Maintain neutrality and objectivity. Be careful about suggestions. Finally, it is also important to remember that only a counselor with training, certification, and experience should implement techniques such as hypnosis and guided imagery. To do otherwise is certainly unethical.

9. Be as open and honest as you can in working with clients and families. Involve your client as often as possible in the documentation process. It can enhance the service relationship, promote empowerment, and make paperwork easier. To know that something is written down and not have any idea what that something is can produce anxiety or inhibition. Clients can cosign entries and be offered the opportunity to write their own notes. It is another method of helping a client develop self-awareness.

Some malpractice suits and accusations of unethical behavior contend a provider gave bad advice or did not tell the client what to expect. Often, discontent lies behind a lawsuit or grievance, and one possible way to keep someone satisfied is to involve him or her in the documentation process. Clients may be less likely to subpoena a record if they know the contents are their words.

Involving the person can also increase a client's understanding before a session is ended. Many times an interview is terminated on the assumption that the patient heard and understood everything. Sometimes, they are overwhelmed with multiple stressors and do not hear or understand. Obviously, involving the client will not work with everyone, but it is an idea you can use more often than you might believe.

NEED FOR SPECIFICITY

As noted in the earlier editions of this monograph, there must be constant awareness of risk management and loss prevention principles. Awareness of ethical principles also applies. To do less increases vulnerability. The plaintiff's attorney is duty bound to be the client's best possible advocate. Your feelings, opinions, and documents are of use only insofar as they contribute to a financial settlement of the client's claim.

The opposition's goal is to establish credibility even if it requires the destruction of your reputation. The validity of your records will be challenged, and information will be reviewed with a fine-toothed comb.

It will be important for you to be able to show that you acted in good faith, within the scope of your job function, and in compliance with your internal standards of care as well as with your code of ethics. Do not provide ammunition to the plaintiff's attorney. Without adequate documentation, credibility and professionalism can easily be questioned.

Before you write a court report, obtain a clear understanding of what is needed and why. Your responsibility to the client is to provide only the requested information. Do not write letters based on what you think someone may want because you might inadvertently violate a client's right to privacy. Do not respond unless the client signed a release or you have a court order. Be sure to retain that release or order in your records.

Intent to harm may or may not have an effect on a jury decision. There are several variables to consider. If, for example, someone is practicing casting with a new fishing rod and does not see you come up behind them, and the hook lands in your arm, you would probably be awarded damages based on the person's negligence, but you would probably not be awarded punitive damages because it was not done with intent to harm. However, if you and the other person had a fight and he or she said with anger, "How does this feel?" and cast the hook directly at you, you could probably obtain a larger settlement. Likewise, if you put information in a letter or a record that may be considered harmful from the client's point of view, then your liability risk is increased. So if you are writing about a client you do not like or may be angry with, be sure your words pertain only to the client's situation and do not reflect your negative attitude(s).

If your letter appears to be speculation rather than a statement of fact or a clearly defined professional opinion, it does a disservice to you, your agency, your client, your profession, and the court. My experience indicates that judges and lawyers prefer clear writing. They like strong verbs, short sentences, use of first person, and positive forms. They do not like abstract nouns, long sentences, hard-to-understand phrases, third person, and negative forms.

Achieving effective communication is a complicated task in every aspect of our society. Other publications about documentation or other trainers may declare specificity is the worst possible thing to include in the record, but I say specificity is absolutely essential.

Vague words can cause problems in every segment of society. Several years ago, there was so much confusion about terms such as *reduced fat* and *low fat* that the federal government had to set national standards so people could know what they were buying. As I was preparing the previous edition of this monograph, I read a newspaper with the following headline: "It's the puzzle of trying to eat right: What's a 'portion'?" According to the reporter, the U.S. government, individual states, and most food manufacturers did not use the same standards or vocabulary. No one could agree about what constitutes a serving. For instance, a muffin was considered a serving, but there was no reference to size or weight, so there was limited value to the term *serving*. The same confusion exists today.

Given that documentation in counseling records must be precise and comprehensive, what happens when counselors are not careful? You may find, as I have, entries like these in client charts:

- "Patty's mother remains deceased at this present time."
- "When eating a sandwich, Sharon will take one bite at a time for 5 days."
- "Rita is some better than the last week. Wednesday she took a little nap on the cat."
- "Larry, age 5, wrote his name on the blackboard exactly backwards. He shows signs of major improvement."
- "Mickey made progress in bed-wetting but not as much as he could have."
- A prescription: "Zantac 300 mg. Take one tablet daily after supper to prevent acid rain at night."
- "Carolyn was apparently born when her mother was only 14."

Seriously, without current and accurate documentation, risk exposure is increased. But please remember, we are talking about minimizing risk, not eliminating it. Decisions must be made on a case-by-case basis, and no single book or workshop will provide you with a fail-safe system of record keeping or ensure ethical conduct. When in doubt, especially in high-risk cases, consult with an attorney.

CHAPTER 9

Terminations

Counselors terminate a counseling relationship when it becomes reasonably apparent that the client no longer needs assistance, is not likely to benefit, or is being harmed by continued counseling. Counselors may terminate counseling when in jeopardy of harm by the client, or another person with whom the client has a relationship, or when clients do not pay fees as agreed upon. Counselors provide pretermination counseling and recommend other service providers when necessary.
—ACA Code of Ethics, A.11.c.

When the work is done, and the case is closed, there is another dimension to counseling that is often forgotten or neglected. The final official piece of documentation in the counseling record is a termination or discharge summary.

The two most obvious reasons for good documentation in the termination summary are (1) a client returns for additional service and/or (2) a client or the client's legal representative initiates a malpractice suit. An increasingly cited basis of a malpractice suit against the counselor is abandonment.

Your termination documentation, like all other sections of the record, must be well written to confirm professional interventions. This chapter includes samples of an actual termination letter and an actual termination summary, analyses of these documents, and suggested rewrites. I encourage you to use these to review your own procedures for writing effective closure documents.

THE TERMINATION LETTER

Original letter, August 22, 2007

Dear Mrs. Monroe:

It has been quite some time since I have seen or heard from you. I would be interested in knowing how you are and if I can be of any further help to you.

Please contact me at 123-4567 by September 14, 2007. If I have not heard from you by then, I will assume that you wish to terminate services.

I look forward to hearing from you in the near future.

[signature/credentials]

Analysis

- *It has been quite some time since I have seen or heard from you.* When was the last service? How long is "quite some time"? What was the nature of the last contact?
- *I would be interested in knowing how you are and if I can be of any further help to you.* This sentence implies the counselor has been a help to the client. Is there a basis for this belief? Does the counselor actually want to serve the client again, or is this a meaningless statement that is included in all letters?
- *Please contact me at 123-4567 by September 14, 2007. If I have not heard from you by then, I will assume that you wish to terminate services. I look forward to hearing from you in the near future.* The letter implies the counselor is looking forward to the client's return. Again, is this remark a common courtesy? What if the counselor did not want the client to return? Why does the counselor assume the client does not want service? Why not state a closure date if no contact?

Suggested Rewrite

Dear Mrs. Monroe:

You have not phoned or kept an appointment since May 12, 2007. This letter is to assure you of our continuing interest in your welfare. Please let me know within the next 3 weeks if you want to return for additional counseling.

My notes reminded me of our discussion about your belief that therapy is not necessary. The choice is yours, but many people have found that regularly scheduled sessions coupled with medication have been helpful to those suffering from depression. I suggest you return to therapy either here or with another community agency of your choice. You may call the regional hotline at 123-4242 if you need emergency or referral services. Your file will be closed if you have not contacted us by October 1. Please understand, however, that you may return at any future date.

[signature / credentials]

THE TERMINATION SUMMARY

Original termination summary for Mrs. Monroe, October 31, 2007

- *Reason for closure:* Client not seen since May 12, 2007.
- *Summary of progress toward goals, including final diagnostic impression:* Clt appeared to make little progress—continues c ^ psychiatric symptoms when uses etoh—denies etoh is problem. Acute depression. Paranoid delusional d/o. Etoh dep.
- *Follow-up plan:* No response to follow-up letter.
- *Other pertinent information:* [This eight-line section of the termination form was left blank.]

Analysis

- *Reason for closure: Client not seen since May 12, 2007.* Was there any outreach between May (date of last appointment) and October (date of this letter)? If yes, were the letters, home visits, and/or phone calls documented? If no, will the chart verify this acutely depressed client was never a danger to herself or others?
- *Summary of progress toward goals including final diagnostic impression: Clt appeared to make little progress.* Is the word *appeared* necessary? Can the phrase *little progress* be defined? What area improved? What problems remained unchanged? How many times was she seen?
- *Continues c ^ psychiatric symptoms when uses etoh—denies etoh is problem. Acute depression. Paranoid.* What symptoms were exhibited? What services were offered? How did the client respond to counseling? Are you sure *denies* is the correct word? Perhaps

she is incapable of denying. Remember how Mr. Johnson, the former client, felt in chapter 5 (A Client's Perspective)? Are the abbreviations understandable?

- *Follow-up plan: No response to follow-up letter.* This is a statement of fact, but it is not a plan.
- *Other pertinent information: This eight-line section of the form was left blank.* Blank spaces create doubt about your ability to obtain clinical information or the genuineness of your interest in the client.

Suggested Rewrite

- *Reason for termination:* Client was seen eight times between March 4, 2005, and May 12, 2007. She did not agree with the judge's referral and stated she did not want counseling because she considers it a waste of time. She did not respond to three messages left on her answering machine or two letters urging her to return to counseling.
- *Summary of progress:* Client seen five times by counselor, two times by psychologist, and once by the psychiatrist. She was delusional and paranoid as evidenced by repeated statements such as, "People are trying to kill me. I can't trust anyone." She would not consider a voluntary hospitalization, and her family was unwilling to consider a mental inquest warrant. No progress.
- *Final diagnostic impression:* 296.3 Major Depressive Disorder Recurrent; 295.30 Schizophrenia (subtype) Paranoid Type; 291.5 Alcohol-Induced Psychotic Disorder, With Delusions.
- *Follow-up plan:* Write letter to assure client of interest and encourage the use of counseling/medication.
- *Other pertinent information:* 42 years old, divorced, two adult children living out of state. Saw Dr. Ralph Stanley, private psychiatrist, and was hospitalized for acute depression in December 2006. Client reported being sexually abused as a child.

It should be obvious from these samples that well-thought-out and detailed closing documentation greatly enhances both the record and the counselor's credibility.

ABANDONMENT

As previously stated, abandonment is increasingly cited as the basis for malpractice suits against counselors. If Mrs. Monroe, as just described, should commit suicide, attempt suicide, or harm or kill another person, abandonment or unethical conduct could be a concern. *Abandonment* is the negligent interruption or termination of services. A counselor's risk exposure increases when

- a client comes to treatment erratically;
- records do not verify outreach efforts to a client who breaks or misses appointments;
- high-risk clients drop out of treatment;
- a client is "fired" or refused service;
- the counselor and client have not discussed and agreed on closure;
- a client is not notified in writing that the case is being closed;
- the record indicates a failure to review, consult, or refer; or
- staff notes do not verify that a plan is being followed.

To reduce the opportunity of being charged with abandonment, here are a few suggestions:

- When you terminate a case, provide the client with a written, factual basis for the closure and keep a copy in the record.
- Be courteous, sincere, and professional. Provide the client with names and phone numbers of other therapists and / or community resources.
- Outline the closure plan with an emphasis on the client's responsibilities after termination.
- Document efforts to contact a client when appointments are not kept.
- Discuss outstanding fees briefly and do not threaten legal action.
- When a client cannot be located, consider notification through a friend or family member. When an agency concludes that a friend or family member should not be notified or when the agency is unable to locate the client, the decision "not to notify" or "unable to notify" should be documented.

The *Code* prohibits abandonment, saying, "Counselors do not abandon or neglect clients in counseling. Counselors assist in making appropriate arrangements for the continuation of treatment, when necessary, during interruptions such as vacations, illness, and following termination" (A.11.a.).

RIGHT TO REFUSE SERVICE

Sometimes a client will not comply with the plan of care, is violent or threatens violence, or for a variety of reasons, is uncooperative. Even though the counselor's intention is to help the individual achieve the highest level of functioning and participate as fully as possible in a satisfying life, such a goal contains some elements that are beyond a counselor's control. There may be occasions when services may be discontinued by the counseling professional. In these cases, refusal to provide service must be carefully and accurately documented, preferably with consultation and signed approval by a supervisor, primary physician, or psychiatrist.

Documentation in the record must verify one or more of the following issues: refusal to take medication as prescribed, a pattern of failure to follow treatment recommendations, violent behavior or threats of violent behavior, repeated canceled or missed appointments, and criminal behavior.

Regardless of the rationale for an involuntary cessation of treatment, a case review should be conducted. If you are in private practice, the review could include other professionals from the community or your own professional organization(s). The review must be documented and include the names and credentials of each participant. A copy of the review could be made available to the client.

When a client or legal guardian cannot or will not participate in the termination process, it is important for the professional to reach out actively to encourage participation, for example, through phone calls and letters. Always document your efforts, and if letters are returned, file them in the chart with the original postmarked envelope.

The issues of termination and right to refuse service should be discussed with a client at the time of an initial assessment unless determined clinically inappropriate. These issues can also be addressed when the permission for service form is signed, or it can be explained in a rights and responsibilities statement or policy that is provided to every client.

In these difficult situations a counselor can always look to the *Code* for guidance. For example, the *Code* says, "If counselors determine an inability to be of professional assistance to clients, they avoid entering or continuing counseling relationships. Counselors are knowledgeable about culturally and clinically appropriate referral resources and suggest these alternatives. If clients decline the suggested referrals, counselors should discontinue the relationship" (A.11.b.).

Doing good isn't bad and it isn't easy either. We are in a tough business and it's getting tougher each day. If you're not feeling stressed out, I don't know why. In fact, I detect a condition I refer to as post-training traumatic syndrome, so, before we proceed, here is one of my songs to treat that condition.

I Need a Respite

Databases and diagnosis,
case reviews and prognosis.
I think I have a new psychosis.
I am buried in a pile of paperwork. I need a respite.

Every few years, it's a brand new game.
That DSM won't stay the same.
If it's ever finished, I'll be insane.
I am buried in a pile of paperwork. I need a respite.

Most staff meetings are a waste of time.
They don't have much reason or rhyme.
Bored and angry, that's what I'm.
I am buried in a pile of paperwork. I need a respite.

Frequently Asked Questions About Documentation

Q: **All I want to do is serve people in need. Paperwork has nothing to do with the quality of my service or the outcome. Why is documentation so important?**

A: Other professionals will need the record for multiple uses. These include, for example, use by

- the primary provider in order to adhere to an established plan of care and assure continuity;
- another staff person in order to assure appropriate intervention when the primary provider is not available;
- the primary provider's supervisor in order to review quality of service and adherence to a plan of care and to evaluate the provider's professional growth;
- the utilization review and quality assurance committee in order to evaluate appropriateness of service, review use of professional time, and examine program effectiveness;
- the state auditor and any other external monitor in order to determine compliance with licensure and/or funding source regulations;
- the plaintiff's attorney in order to educate the jury by pointing out missing dates, changed dates, wrong dates, missing notes or plans, vague entries, and inconsistent or conflicting information; and
- a board of inquiry in order to evaluate compliance with the code of ethics.

Q: If my documentation is subpoenaed, what options do I have?

A: The best direction will be obtained from a lawyer. Nevertheless, here are several suggestions:

- You should verify the validity of a subpoena or court order.
- You should make sure you have appropriate client consent or have called the client's attorney to see if he or she will file a motion to quash the subpoena.
- You may be able to submit a duplicate client record that has been certified as correct, or you may be required to appear in court to testify. Less staff time is used when a certified record is provided, but there is no opportunity for the counselor to offer clarification.
- If you are permitted and choose to submit a certified copy, it is important to hand deliver the material only to the individual specified on the subpoena and obtain a receipt or use certified mail with return receipt service. The certification form should contain, at least, the following information: name and signature of the record custodian; name, signature, and seal of a notary public; name and identification number of subpoenaed record; the total number of pages being copied; name, address, and phone number of the organization that provided services; and a statement such as, "I certify that the attached copies are a true and complete reproduction of the original documentation. This certification is provided in lieu of a personal appearance."
- If you are required to appear in person, do not permit examination of the documentation and do not give up possession of counseling records until instructed to do so by the judge.
- Do not fabricate documentation especially for the purpose of a particular proceeding.

Q: Is it wise to keep two records, that is, the primary record for everyday use and an unofficial chart that contains personal notations and client statements or information that others would use for negative reasons?

A: Although some state laws may immunize personal notes from discovery, in my opinion, it is not wise to keep two sets of records. To do so is actually creating more paperwork. I recall one workshop participant telling me about a separate record that was written in a foreign language to prevent others from accessing client information. That is not absolute protection because other people can read foreign languages. In addition, anything that is discoverable, depending upon the nature of the case, might be ordered into court. If you are successful in keeping the existence of such records a secret but are called into court, you may be asked if you have provided all pertinent records. To lie about the existence of other information is perjury and a violation of ethics.

In a related matter, I recall another person telling me about staff who were instructed to write so illegibly that no one could read clinical entries. The thinking was the records could not be used against staff. I suggest you maintain one legible, current, understandable, and comprehensive record.

Q: **What relationship do brochures and flyers have to documentation in the record?**

A: Printed materials are promises to your clients and your community. Therefore, they must be accurate descriptions of staff qualifications, services offered, and anything else you want someone to know. Do not make promises that cannot be kept. Additionally, the flyer will tell you what needs to be in the counseling record. If the flyer states, for example, that each client will have an individualized plan of care developed by a multidisciplinary treatment team consisting of counselor, psychologist, nurse, social worker, case manager, and psychiatrist, then it is necessary to have such a plan in every record. I frequently read records that do not list any staff name other than the person who wrote the plan. Some may contain the cosignature of a supervisor or a psychiatrist, but there is no evidence they actually participated in the development of the plan or case review. If the brochure indicates that the staff has special qualifications or lists credentials, licenses, and certifications, then charts must be signed by staff members who have earned such credentials.

When advertising materials indicate the availability of emergency or after-hour services, they must be available. And when these services are provided, the clinical entry should be labeled as such.

If a brochure indicates there will be an opportunity for the client to assess and strengthen vocational skills (or whatever), a record must verify the client's participation throughout the counseling process.

When the material provides information about success rates, your office should have a separate and current file with information that confirms such claims (e.g., reduced alcohol/drug-related offenses, job retention rates, successful short-term therapy for marital discord, fewer hospitalizations).

If the literature states a client will be seen within a specific number of hours or days, an overview of your records must be able to confirm it happens. How would it look if the record showed a high-risk client called for an appointment on April 9, overdosed in a suicide attempt on April 13, but was not scheduled to be seen until April 30?

Q: Does every staff note, treatment plan, case review, and letter have to be original? I could save time if forms and letters were preprinted.

A: Clinical forms can be partially preprinted, but every form must contain some handwritten information that has not been preprinted (e.g., observations, opinions, client responses). Any signatures should also be original.

Form letters could be prepared for a variety of purposes, including but not limited to appointment confirmation or cancellation, missed appointments, responses to requests for information, attempts to contact a client, and thank-you notes to a referral source. The signature, however, should be original.

Q: My clients use slang and vulgar language. Should I use their words in the record?

A: The record is a professional document, primarily maintained to ensure appropriate treatment. As such, it must contain information that you or another must rely on to optimize quality care and risk management prevention. It is important to provide an accurate picture of the person being served, but it is not necessary to fill a record with slang and vulgarities. Perhaps you could quote the individual on one occasion and then cross-reference future entries to this specific date for an example of inappropriate or vulgar language.

Q: **Should client information be faxed?**

A: A patient's right to privacy is compromised each time information is faxed. Unless the situation is critical (i.e., life and death), the use of fax machines is discouraged. There is a major breach of confidentiality should the information be accidentally received by an unintended person. If you fax, the transmission must contain a cover letter to a specific individual stating that the information is confidential, intended for use only by that person, and that receipt must be acknowledged. The cover letter must let an unintended reader know that dissemination of said material is prohibited. Finally, the letter should contain the name, address, phone number, and fax number of the sender with a request for the unintended recipient to immediately notify the sender. The original cover letter and acknowledgment of receipt are filed in the counseling record.

Q: **May I terminate services to a client who will not pay for counseling, and how should such a termination be documented?**

A: Ideally, service will be terminated when it is no longer required or when it does not or cannot meet the client's needs. It is also best when you and the client make a termination decision together. Whatever the particular circumstances, they must be carefully documented in the record.

   Clients who need services must not be abandoned, and in such cases, service must be withdrawn only in unusual circumstances. Make every effort to minimize possible adverse effects, offer assistance in making appropriate arrangements, and document each of these steps in the record.

Professionals who are in a fee-for-service setting may terminate service to clients who do not pay if the monetary arrangements were made clear, in writing, to the client before service began; if the client does not pose an imminent danger to self or others; and if the consequences of nonpayment have been discussed and documented in the chart (for more information, see chapter 9)

Q: **What can be done about entries that were never written or entries that were written but cannot be found?**

A: Several factors must be considered. Is the case active or closed? Is the counselor an employee or a former employee? How long has the information been missing or lost?

- *Missing items in documentation:* If the counselor is still an employee, entries should be made within 24 hours of the discovery or at the counselor's earliest opportunity. Documentation must list actual service date(s) and the date of the belated entry. If a long period of time has elapsed since the entry should have been made, all the counselor can do is indicate that the belated entry represents his or her best memory of what occurred.

  If the counselor is no longer an employee, every effort should be made to contact the provider in order to have him or her write entries within a reasonable time of the discovery. If the counselor cannot be located or fails to submit the missing data, another professional can make an entry to explain the situation. Documentation must list actual service date(s), the date of the belated entry, and an explanation. If the client is active, he or she should be informed of the situation, sign another permission to treat form, and perhaps be allowed to read and cosign late entries. If these entries have been subpoenaed and there is no way to contact the former employee, the court should be notified that documentation is not available but that another professional can testify from existing entries that are filed in the chart, or from memory if there is personal knowledge of the client's situation.

- *Missing records (entire chart):* If the counselor is still an employee, entries should be made within 24 hours of the discovery. The new file should be labeled *Replacement Record.* Documentation must explain that the original folder was lost and specify the date range that is being addressed from memory. Also list the dates of the belated entries. If the lost record has been subpoenaed, the court should be notified that documentation is not available but the professional can testify from memory.

  If the counselor is no longer an employee, every effort should be made to contact the provider in order to have him or her write entries within a reasonable time of the discovery. If the counselor cannot be located or fails to submit the missing data, another professional can make an entry to explain the situation. Documentation must list actual service date(s), the date of the belated entry, and an entry to explain the situation. The new file should be labeled *Replacement Record.* Documentation must explain that the original folder was lost and indicate the specific date range that is being addressed from memory. Also list the date that the belated entries were made. If the client is active, he or she should be informed of the situation, sign another permission to treat form, and perhaps be allowed to read and cosign late entries. If these entries have been subpoenaed, the court should be notified that documentation is not available but that another professional can testify from existing entries that were filed in the chart and from memory.

Q: Please comment on filing systems and security.

A: Records should be used on the day of service delivery and returned to a storage area at day's end. It is also important to document when a chart is removed from the records department. This can be accomplished through the use of a sign-out slip. The person who signed out the chart becomes responsible for its security.

Every effort should be made to ensure that charts are not taken out of the building. If records are used outside the office, there must be a specific policy and there must be compliance with that policy.

Care should also be taken to ensure that records are not left in view in unattended offices. When you are going to be out of the office and there is a remote possibility that someone could enter the office and see client information, the chart should be locked in a desk.

Some charts, usually substance abuse charts, must be filed and secured in accordance with federal regulations. Certain other records may also need special procedures (e.g., Employee Assistance Program charts, records of an employee's family member, records of a locally prominent person). All charts should be maintained under the supervision of an office manager. If you are in a small, private practice, then you also may be the office manager, and therefore all responsibilities for document security are yours.

Q: Why are cosignatures important?

A: A cosignature serves as confirmation of training or supervision. Students completing a field placement should have all entries cosigned, and the cosigner must accept the legal, ethical, and clinical implications of his or her signature. This is not an issue to be taken lightly.

Some states and some funding sources will accept only the signature of a "recognized," "covered," or "qualified" professional. Each state is different, so it is your responsibility to find out what is required. Professionals with some bachelor's and some master's degrees may not be acceptable as primary care providers or as supervisors. Usually, a professional with a state license or certification is acceptable.

If supervision was not provided, the note should not be cosigned simply to obtain reimbursement. To do so is unethical and illegal.

Each time anyone in the organization provides a service or has direct contact with a client or the client's legal representative, there is a risk. The risk is more complicated when that

someone is a student or a volunteer. Not only can these individuals be hurt on the job, but they can also render a service
that results in a lawsuit. In addition, there are financial considerations, because students and volunteers, in most instances,
may not bill for their services. And finally, it is important to
understand labor laws that could restrict their activities. The
Department of Labor may recognize some individuals as exempt from Fair Labor Standards, but it is your responsibility to
know and to comply.

If students and volunteers provide counseling, their level of
education and previous experience (if any) must verify that
they are qualified to be working with clients, especially if the
client has a history of hospitalizations or any behavior pattern
that might be construed as high risk. Volunteers and students
can be positive components of quality programming; however,
the best strategy is to prevent an incident that leads to a lawsuit, a repayment, or allegations of unethical conduct.

Q: What record-keeping guidelines are there for dealing with HIV clients?

A: Unfortunately, there is not much legal guidance in terms of
what to document or not document with regard to clients with
HIV / AIDS. As noted in the first edition of this monograph,
you should probably lean toward protecting the client's right
to confidentially. A lawyer once told me, "Whichever way you
go, you are deciding which lawsuit you want to face." Another attorney told me that serious problems could arise from
failure to document information about HIV / AIDS. She said
a diagnosis of HIV / AIDS is extremely traumatic and will
certainly be relevant to the mental health of any client. Since
the counseling record is the means by which you document
care and understanding of the client, meaningful entries are
critical to treatment decisions. Failure to document such a
major concern in the client's life could lead to malpractice. In
a sense, the omission of this important information provides
some level of confidentiality for the client, but it is a poor
way to protect yourself.

The fact that you do not write what you know does not eliminate the fact that you know something. Problems most often result from failure to document rather than from making an entry. In all likelihood, you will not protect yourself by not writing, especially if a client says something like, "I have AIDS and I don't care if I pass it on. If fact, I hope I can pass it on to (the specific name of a person who shares sex and/or needles)."

A counselor's most pressing ethical predicament, of course, is having knowledge about HIV/AIDS and not knowing where the client's right to privacy ends and the right to know begins for any exposed individuals, inclusive of, but not limited to, the client's sexual partner(s) or someone who shares needles. Every situation is unique and will require a review with a lawyer. It must also be understood that this monograph is not a substitute for legal advice. In no event is the American Counseling Association or the author liable for damages that may result from the use of any information contained in this publication.

There will always be ethical dilemmas. Some issues are never resolved to everyone's satisfaction, and I believe the right to privacy versus the right to know will always be one of those issues. You understand the sensitivity of confidential information; all you can do is your best to protect it. It will take constant effort, but don't ever give up.

The wise counselor will always turn to the *Code* for assistance in making difficult decisions. Two sections are particularly relevant:

1. "The general requirement that counselors keep information confidential does not apply when disclosure is required to protect clients or identified others from serious and foreseeable harm or when legal requirements demand that confidential information must be revealed. Counselors consult with other professionals when in doubt as to the validity of an exception" (B.2.a.).
2. "When clients disclose that they have a disease commonly known to be both communicable and life threatening, counselors may be justified in disclosing information to identifiable third parties, if they are known to be at demonstrable

and high risk of contracting the disease. Prior to making a disclosure, counselors confirm that there is such a diagnosis and assess the intent of clients to inform the third parties about their disease or to engage in any behaviors that may be harmful to an identifiable third party" (B.2.b.).

Q: What legal security is offered by a disclaimer form?

A: Any form can be questioned, but there is some value in a disclaimer form because it is confirmation that the counselor made an effort to advise a client of risk. No form will provide unlimited and total protection, but you are encouraged to have forms that specify risk and verify the client's informed consent.

The best kind of disclaimer is one that informs the client of possible risks in order to permit an informed decision. Although the form can be important, it is more important to make sound clinical decisions relative to the risk involved. Is a proposed event on or off agency property? Will you or another employee provide transportation in a personal automobile? Will clients drive themselves or others? Is the event necessary (listed in the treatment plan) or is it simply encouraged? How old is the client? Is he or she legally able to sign a consent or disclaimer form? Is the event inside or outside? What physical activity is involved? Obviously, for persons with disabilities, there are different risks for a hike in the woods and sitting in a theater. Common sense and good clinical judgment are required. If a picnic is held 25 miles from the office and seven clients (two of whom have a history of violent and aggressive behavior) are in an auto designed for five passengers, and if a volunteer or student is driving, risk exposure has been increased and the value of a disclaimer form is diminished. All events must be evaluated for clinical appropriateness and safety. Is it possible to substitute another activity with less risk but equal treatment value? Will clients or guardians be given the opportunity to decline participation? Is all of this being documented?

Disclaimers can improve patient–client communication and encourage both parties to use precautionary measures. Therefore, liability shields can also be an effective management tool. However, the form must address specific concerns in a specific time frame. A liability disclaimer form should include the following text and information:

1. My participation at (name activity) is voluntary. I understand the event is not required but can assist me in the attainment of treatment goals I agree with. No liability will be imposed upon (name of individual or organization) for any injury that I may sustain. Should emergency treatment be required, I authorize said service. I have read and understand the content and intent of this form and acknowledge consent by my signature.
2. Client signature and date
3. Parent or guardian signature and date, if needed
4. Witness signature and date.

Finally, liability shields will never provide protection from criminal behavior or unethical behavior.

Q: Please comment on HIPAA regulations.

A: The Health Insurance Portability and Accountability Act of 1996 is one of the lengthiest and most complex pieces of legislation passed by the United States Congress. Prior to HIPAA, there were no standard measures to address all aspects of the security of stored or transmitted electronic information. According to the HIPAA Web site (www.Hipaaadvisory.com), "The purpose of HIPAA is to adopt national standards for safeguards to protect the confidentiality, integrity, and availability of electronically protected health information."

In other words, care providers must assure clients that the integrity, confidentiality, and availability of health information they collect, maintain, use, or transmit are protected. Nevertheless, there are some basic facts you need to know.

Many of the regulations do not relate to patient management but rather to national standards for security, privacy, and electronic transactions and transaction data code sets, specifically the use of *The International Classification of Mental and Behavioral Disorders: Clinical Descriptions and Diagnosis Guidelines* (*ICD-10;* World Health Organization, 2003).

Two primary issues addressed are the following:

1. The Privacy Rule relates to all protected information in any medium (written, oral, or electronic). This rule is most relevant to this monograph because it is designed to give the consumer or patient more control over the record's content, as it relates to him or her. Patients and consumers have the following rights:

   - To be informed about the privacy practices—this means they must be given a written notice of privacy practices.
   - To object to or limit use and disclosure of personally identifiable health information.
   - To review a designated record set—there are numerous interpretations about what constitutes a designated record set, so you must discuss your specific concerns with a HIPAA expert.
   - To request amendment of information
   - To know to whom information has been disclosed

2. The Security Standard (wireless, wires, and paper) requires a policy and procedure related to

   - access to patient information;
   - the capability of capturing and reporting all consents and authorizations (and absences of consents and authorizations) granted by a client or patient;
   - the capability of tracking and managing HIPAA complaints and requests;
   - the security of the electronic client record and information that is transmitted by e-mail, e-mail readers such as RIM's Blackberry, cell phones, pagers, and faxes;
   - the capability of handling problems related to electronic downtime, termination of service (electronic or otherwise), and hackers (encryption is required when information is transmitted over the Web);

- the nature and amount of transmitted content, meaning clinical, administrative, and fiscal information, as well as who receives it; and
- the use of mobile technology and remote access.

Your best course of action is to consult with a lawyer or recognized expert before implementing a policy and procedure.

Q: Our job is difficult and often misunderstood. Some people just want to use records against us. Why should we expose ourselves to risk day after day?

A: Because it is a worthy endeavor to care for another human being and help others achieve self-sufficiency and happiness. For further thoughts on this question, refer to the Epilogue: You Make a Difference.

What Would You Do?: Ethical Considerations

This section of the book is meant to serve only as a vehicle for discussion. As such, it contains a series of brief questions and briefer guidelines for resolution. I encourage you to consider your own possible answers, to discuss the answers with colleagues, and to encourage opportunities for agency-wide discussions of these and other ethical and procedural questions. My brief answers represent my own views based on my experiences and understanding of the *Code.* Certainly, your answers may differ from or expand upon mine.

SCENARIOS FOR DISCUSSION
AND PROFESSIONAL DEVELOPMENT

Q: What would you do if your personal ethics conflicted with your agency policies or relevant state or federal laws?

A: Make an effort to resolve the dispute in a manner that is consistent with the *Code.* Simple answers are not always available to resolve complex issues; therefore, it is always best to seek other opinions. Albert Einstein said, "Problems cannot be solved by the same level of thinking that created them."

Discuss the issue with someone in a position of authority, and if the problem cannot be worked out internally, you may have to consider consulting a mediator or, as a last resort, leaving the agency. During my 43-year career, I left two agencies because of philosophical and/or ethical differences.

Q: What would you do if the local court ordered a man to see you for a substance abuse assessment, but when you see him, you realize he was a former classmate you occasionally shared social drinks with?

Q: What would you do if you were assigned to complete a referral for a disability evaluation and the client who walks into your office is a cousin?

Q: What would you do if you were involved in a difficult case involving allegations of sexual abuse, and as you complete the initial intake, you realize you purchased a car from the alleged perpetrator's father 2 years ago?

A: Refer the individual to a competent colleague to avoid a dual relationship.

Q: What would you do if a former boyfriend or girlfriend came to the office after a divorce to request your evaluation of his or her son for the purpose of a custody recommendation?

A: This happened to an associate of mine who immediately referred the client to another professional, requested client records be kept in an alternate, locked location so there would be no opportunity to look at them, and excused himself from staff discussions related to the case. These actions are an excellent example of ethical conduct.

Q: What would you do if a client asked you to join him or her for a cup of coffee, a lunch, or a sporting event?

A: Most professionals know they should not date or have intimate relationships with clients, but some interactions might be appropriate. For example, a counselor or job coach needs to observe and evaluate a client's interactions before placing him or her on the job. However, some social scenarios can also send the wrong message to a client. One professional recalled how clients asked why she did not stop and speak to them at church or the mall. She explained that her policy is to be polite and greet the individual with "Hello, how are you?" but she does not consent to lengthy conversations outside of the professional domain. She believes this approach is more respectful to the clients and also acknowledges her right to private time.

Q: **What would you do if you were directed to write a brochure that exaggerated the truth and thereby increased referrals to the agency?**

A: Do not inflate statistics in order to make a program appear more effective than it is. One agency released a paper that claimed an unusually high rate of success, but a closer review of program statistics confirmed that unmotivated clients were simply terminated or not accepted into the program. This one is easy. Marketing material must be factual.

Nevertheless, in my collection of agency brochures, one flyer contains this statement: "Does anyone need to know? Our services are completely confidential." The implication is that no one will have access to client information and, as we know, that is not completely true. There will always be court orders, peer reviews, and funding source audits. Another agency brochure contains a list of client rights including this one: "Information is confidential. No information is released without your signed permission." Although it is important to advise clients we do our best to protect their information, statements like this are, in fact, misrepresentations and deceptive (and, therefore, a violation of the code of ethics).

Q: **What would you do if you needed to increase your monthly service and revenue statistics?**

A: Unfortunately, deception can be found within the helping professions. Consider the following news story: Social service and health care scams may be costing a variety of funding sources $100 million a day. One unethical system involved an agency that billed for phony services by obtaining client signatures on blank claim forms, thus allowing them to provide unnecessary services and/or bill for interventions that were not rendered. In another case, the counseling professional billed for services even though a coworker with fewer credentials actually provided the services. The coworker also wrote the staff notes, but the more qualified professional signed the note in order to obtain a higher rate of reimbursement. We can legitimately say these are exceptions to the rule, but these exceptions receive wide public attention and help form public opinion. The *Code* contains specific instructions: "Counselors are accurate, honest, and objective in reporting their professional activities and judgments to appropriate third parties, including courts, health insurance companies, those who are the recipients of evaluation reports, and others" (C.6.b.).

Q: What would you do to get a job you wanted?

A: Employment must be accepted only on the basis of existing competence or the prospective employer's agreement to allow you to acquire the necessary competence. In fact, that's how I got my first job. I had a B.A. in sociology but needed a master's in social work. The child welfare agency hired me at full salary and permitted me to study full time during the 2-year program. In exchange, I worked weekends and holidays during the school year, and after I obtained a master's, I worked for the agency for 2 years.

Q: What would you do if you had the opportunity to make your life more comfortable at the expense of clients or an organization?

A: Safeguard the resources of your employer by conserving funds when possible and do not misappropriate funds or use them for unintended or unauthorized purposes. If, for example, you have authority to disperse funds or services, allocate resources according to policy, not according to a favorite project or person. Do not buy a $600 chair when a $300 chair meets agency needs. Do not inflate mileage reports. Do not take office supplies home for personal use. If you are being paid to work an 8-hour day, work an 8-hour day. Do not provide excessively expensive meals or snacks for meetings. Do not make a habit of long social visits with coworkers. Adhere to agency policy related to personal phone calls on office time. Repay the agency for the cost of personal long-distance calls unless your employer has authorized them. Adhere to your employer's policy related to the use of the Internet on office time. If there is no policy, use of the Internet should be limited to breaks or mealtimes. A professional is not acting in an ethical manner when company time is used for such activities as personal e-mails, sending jokes to friends, shopping online, or playing fantasy football. Surfing for porn sites is certainly unethical, yet some employees in one state were fired because audits of their computer use confirmed such activity.

Certainly some of these actions seem like small errors in judgment compared to the volume of services rendered by the counselor, but they all contribute to overall ethical behavior.

Q: What would you do if you became dissatisfied with your job or your life?

A: As I was preparing this monograph edition, a newspaper article explained how one person rationalized office behavior by saying, "Wasting time at work is a game played by the unhappy." The article said many employees despised their jobs, and one interviewee said, "I spend my time this way because I am soooooooooo [sic] underpaid. This is extra compensation from me to me. That's how miserable I am."

No one knows the exact number of employees who feel this way, but one news article indicated that 34% of American workers have considered quitting their jobs because of stress. A counselor's discontent will most certainly affect patient care. Such an emotional state is not healthy for you, and it is not helpful for the clients you want to help or coworkers who are depending on you to bear your share of the workload. The ethical thing to do is to get help for yourself. Section C (Professional Responsibility) of the *ACA Code of Ethics* is emphatic on this point, saying that counselors must maintain and promote their emotional and physical well-being by engaging in self-care activities designed to assist them in meeting all professional duties.

SIX STEPS FOR THE RESOLUTION OF ETHICAL PROBLEMS

1. Refer to your code of ethics because it has been designed to provide established, approved, and acceptable standards.
2. If the code does not address the specific issue or if sections of it seem to provide conflicting guidance, then identify the indi-

viduals, groups, and organizations likely to be affected by the action; list possible courses of action with benefits and risks; examine the reasons for and against your action or decision; and ask yourself, "What is the worst possible scenario if the action occurs?"

3. If you have doubts, trust your intuitions and do not act until you consult with colleagues, experts, or an attorney.
4. Document the decision-making process.
5. Make your final decision.
6. Evaluate, and document, the results.

If the situation requires immediate response and if consultation is not possible, follow the steps just listed (but without consultation), make your decision, evaluate the results, and document the reasons that eliminated the possibility for consultation.

CONCLUDING THOUGHTS

Integrity is the foundation of everything discussed in this monograph, because integrity means promotion of the highest values of our professions through study, self-evaluation, and conduct. It also means we contribute time and professional expertise to activities that promote respect for the integrity of our professions by teaching, supervising, providing legislative testimony, making presentations in the community, participating in our professional organizations, and offering workshops at staff meetings or conferences.

The Dalai Lama (1999), in his book *Ethics for the New Millennium*, reminds us that when our actions place service to others above service to self, the possibility of unethical behavior is reduced. He says, "When we act to fulfill our immediate desires without taking into account others' interests, we undermine the possibility for lasting happiness" (p. 53). He later adds that "compassion is one of the principal things that makes our lives meaningful. It is the source of all lasting happiness and joy . . . the foundation of a good heart, the heart of one who acts out of a desire to help others" (p. 234). In my opinion, the words of the Dali Lama are also an accurate description of an ethical counselor.

Epilogue:
You Make a Difference

Ethics training cannot ensure the use of good judgment and ethical conduct. Judgment and conduct, however, are the focus of this monograph. I have attempted to share information and my own experiences that may help protect your clients, yourself, your agency, your profession, and society. We can all ask, "What if? What if?" but as has been pointed out, no training program or book will give you every solution to every problem. In part, I also hope to have motivated you to make a conscious effort every day to do your best. What does that mean? It means at the end of a workday you look in the mirror and ask yourself, "Did I do my best? Nothing illegal. Nothing immoral. And nothing unethical." If you can say yes, then sleep well because no one deserves a good night's sleep more than you. You have seen how newspapers chronicle one ethical problem after another. Every day we see examples of unethical behavior, and often several stories on the same day. Thank goodness most of the stories are not about us. Let's keep it that way. I am proud of my profession, and I am proud of you. I thank you for what you give and what you do every day.

Until we meet again or for the first time, be kind to yourself and remember you are an important person. You may not always believe it, but it's true. You make a difference every day. A rock thrown in the water cannot know about the ripples it will make. You are more than a rock, and you, too, will make ripples that affect other lives.

In fact, people you have never met can have an impact on your life. Let me tell you a story. My wife and I went out for dinner. We were seated next to a table with a young man and his two children, a girl about 8 and a boy about 5. The father was talking, mostly with the son, about responsible behavior, and the father was quite good, just the right amount of warmth and support. The child, however, was 5 years old and not interested in that kind of discussion. I did not think the boy was paying attention to his father, when out of nowhere, the child looked at his father and said, "You know what the problem is? All I need is a bigger box of crayons."

About that time a waitress placed their dinners on the table, and they shared a meal they probably do not remember. However, it is a meal my wife and I will never forget. Years have gone by, yet even today, when either of us is upset about something, the other one says, "All you need is a bigger box of crayons." We both laugh, and for a moment, things do not seem quite as bad. The father and son will never know about their influence on us or about the joy they put in our lives. You, too, will affect other lives. Sometimes you will know about it and sometimes you will not. The people you influence may not know it was something you said or did, but someday, somewhere, there will be a change in a thought process or a pattern of behavior. No one can say with certainty just when a change will occur or how long it will last. But I am convinced that the quality of another life is going to be better because of you. The next time you doubt that you make a difference, remember this story. And, if necessary, get yourself a bigger box of crayons.

One of my favorite movies is the musical version of *Goodbye Mr. Chips*. As the movie ends, an aging teacher reviews his life and wonders if he made a difference in the lives of his students. He sings a song that says, in part, "In the evening of my life I shall look to the sunset . . . and the question I shall ask, only I can answer. Was I brave and strong and true? Did I fill the world with love my whole life through?" Years from now, I believe the world will be a better place because you are here today filling it with love and professional help. I thank you for that and want to share the words of a song I sometimes use to conclude my workshop.

The Good Fight

If you're at the desk by the stroke of eight,
You know for sure that you're not late.
Tomorrow is an audit from the state.
So before you leave don't forget to dictate.
I work everyday to motivate
But first there are strengths to evaluate
And feelings to translate.
Sometimes, I alleviate, formulate, educate, facilitate
or take a much needed break for some chocolate.
Then I return to elucidate,
Negotiate, or tabulate
And when the day ends, it's very late.
Much of life seems disproportionate
As we try to habilitate those who deteriorate.
So I'll give it to you straight.
Your challenge is the ultimate.
But you're fighting the good fight,
So hang in there and be proud!

References, Suggested Readings, and Web Sites

This monograph is based on 40-plus years of experience and countless numbers of books, articles, discussions, and workshops. It is impossible to credit each source of information in this book. However, the following references may be useful.

REFERENCES AND SUGGESTED READINGS

Amatayakul, M. (2004). *Guide to HIPAA auditing: Practical tools and tips to ensure compliance*. Marblehead, MA: hcPro.

Amatayakul, M. (2001). *HIPAA made simple: A practical guide to compliance*. Marblehead, MA: hcPro.

American Association for Marriage and Family Therapy. (2001). *AAMFT code of ethics*. Washington, DC: Author.

American Counseling Association. (2005). *ACA code of ethics*. Alexandria, VA: Author. (Note: Full text is available on the ACA Web site at www.counseling.org/ethics)

American Psychiatric Association. (2000). *Diagnostic and statistical manual of mental disorders* (4th ed., text rev.). Washington, DC: Author.

Campbell, C. D., & Gordon, M. C. (2003). Acknowledging the inevitable: Understanding multiple relationships in rural practice. *Professional Psychology: Research and Practice, 34*(4), 430–434.

Coleman, C. E., & Joseph, A. H. (2001). *HIPAA self-assessment and planning: A guide to the privacy and security standards* (2nd ed.). Marblehead, MA: Opus Communications.

Corey, G., Crey, M. S., & Callanan, P. (2003). *Issues and ethics in the helping professions* (6th ed.). Pacific Grove, CA: Brooks/Cole.

Dalai Lama, the Fourteenth. (1999). *Ethics for the new millennium.* New York: Riverside Books.

Forester-Miller, H., & Rubenstein, R. L. (1992). *Group counseling: Ethics and professional issues.* In D. Capuzzi & D. R. Gross (Eds.), *Introduction to group counseling* (pp. 307–323). Denver, CO: Love.

Herlihy, B., & Corey, G. (2006). *ACA ethical standards casebook* (6th ed.). Alexandria, VA: American Counseling Association.

Herlihy, B., & Corey, G. (2006). *Boundary issues in counseling* (2nd ed.). Alexandria, VA: American Counseling Association.

'Integrity' tops online dictionary's inquiries. (2005, December 11). *Louisville (Kentucky) Courier Journal,* p. A7.

Jackson, V., & Lopez, L. (Eds.). (1999). *Cultural competency in managed behavioral healthcare.* Dover, NH: Odyssey Press.

Joint Commission on Accreditation of Healthcare Organizations. (2001). *Protecting confidentiality: Joint Commission resources.* Oakbrook Terrace, IL: Author.

Jongsma, A. E., Peterson, L. M., & McInnis, W. P. (1996). *The child and adolescent psychotherapy treatment planner.* New York: Wiley.

Kagle, J. D. (1993). Record keeping: Direction for the1990s. *Social Work, 38*(2), 192–196. (Note: This author was a major influence and started me on a record-keeping training journey that has lasted over 20 years. In addition, Ms. Kagle was supportive of my earliest training efforts.)

Lee, C. C. (Ed.). (2006). *Multicultural issues in counseling: New approaches to diversity* (3rd ed.). Alexandria, VA: American Counseling Association.

Luepker, E., & Norton, L. (2002). *Record keeping in psychotherapy and counseling: Protecting confidentiality and the professional relationship.* New York: Brunner-Routledge.

Mitchell, R. W. (1991). *Documentation in counseling records* (ACA Legal Series, Vol. 2). Alexandria, VA: American Counseling Association. (Note: No longer in print.)

Mitchell, R. W. (2001). *Documentation in counseling records* (2nd ed. ACA Legal Series). Alexandria, VA: American Counseling Association.

National Association of Social Workers. (1999). *NASW code of ethics.* Washington, DC: Author.

Pack-Brown, S. P., & Williams, C. B. (2003). *Ethics in a multicultural context.* Thousands Oaks, CA: Sage.

Pedersen, P. B. (2000). *A handbook for developing multicultural awareness* (3rd ed.). Alexandria, VA: American Counseling Association.

Reamer, F. G. (1991). AIDS, social work, and the duty to protect. *Social Work, 36*(1), 56–60.

Reamer, F. G. (2001) *The social work ethics audit: A risk management tool.* Washington, DC: NASW Press.

Reamer, F. G. (2005). Documentation in social work: Evolving ethical and risk management standards. *Social Work, 50*(4), 325–334.

Remley, T. P., Jr., & Herlihy, B. (2005). *Ethical, legal, and professional issues in counseling* (2nd ed.). New York: Prentice Hall. (Note: Ted Remley, attorney and former editor of the ACA Legal Series, attended my record-keeping workshop and was exceedingly supportive of my earliest training efforts. It was Mr. Remley who requested I write my first monograph for ACA, *Documentation in Counseling Records.*)

Sue, D. W., & Sue, D. (2003). *Counseling the culturally diverse: Theory and practice.* New York: Wiley.

Tarasoff v. [California] Board of Regents, 551 p. 2d 334 (1976).

Teresa Vasquez individually, and as personal representative of the estate of Ramon Vasquez v. Ramachandra Kolluru, MD, Albertsons Pharmacy, and Thomas Updike. (1999, October 11). *Blue Sheet of West Texas.*

Thornton, M. (1999). *Ahead of the game: Compliance strategies for the behavioral health industry.* Rockville, MD: National Council of Community Behavioral Healthcare.

Wheeler, A., & Bertram, B. (2007). *The counselor, ethics, and the law* (5th ed.). Alexandria, VA: American Counseling Association.

World Health Organization. (2003). *The international classification of mental and behavioral disorders: Clinical descriptions and diagnosis guidelines (ICD-10).* Geneva, Switzerland: Author.

WEB SITES

American Association of Homes and Services for the Aging
www.aahsa.org

American Association of Marriage and Family Therapy
www.aamft.org

American Counseling Association
   www.counseling.org
American Health Lawyers Association
   www.healthlawyers.org
American Medical Association
   www.ama-assn.org/
   (Contains a free, downloadable booklet on HIPAA, including a
   decision tree for determining whether a practice or covered
   entity must comply with HIPAA.)
American Nurses Association
   www.nursingworld.org
American Psychiatric Association
   www.psych.org
American Psychological Association
   www.apa.org
Child Welfare League of America
   www.cwla.org
hcPro
   www.hcpro.com
Health Care Financing Administration (Medicaid and Medicare
   regulations)
   www.hcfa.org
Health Insurance Portability and Accountability Act
   www.hipaa.org/
Health Insurance Portability and Accountability Act
   www.Hipaaadvisory.com
   (Contains complete regulations and a summary analysis of the
   Security Rule by Tom Grove.)
Health Privacy
   www.healthprivacy.org
Joint Commission on Accreditation of Healthcare Organizations
   www.jointcommission.org
Mitchell, R. W. (author of this monograph)
   http://home.bellsouth.net/p/PWP-bobmitchell
National Association of Qualified Mental Retardation Professionals
   www.qmrp.org
National Association of Social Workers
   www.naswdc.org

National Council for Community Behavioral Healthcare
www.nccbh.org
United States Department of Health and Human Services
(HIPAA information)
http://aspe.hhs.gov/admnsimp/
United States Psychiatric Rehabilitation Association
(formerly known as the International Association of
Psycho-social Rehabilitation)
www.usPRA.org